LANCASHIRE

Hurstwood, a tiny hamlet of Tudor manors and cottages

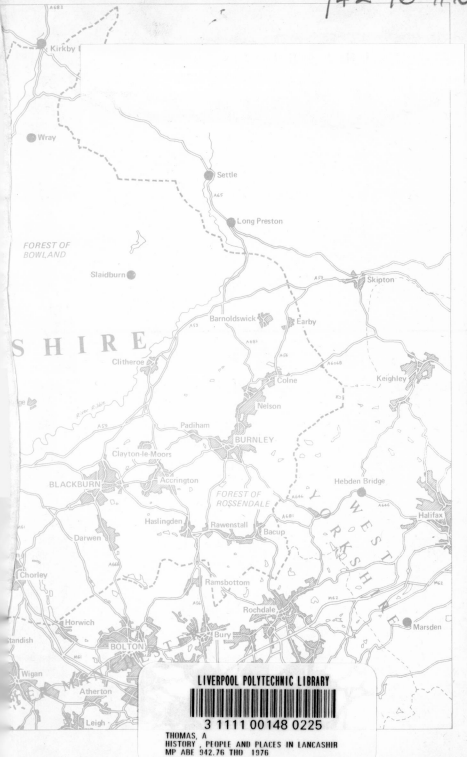

History, People and Places in

LANCASHIRE

Ann Thomas

SPURBOOKS LIMITED

PUBLISHED BY
SPURBOOKS LTD
6 PARADE COURT
BOURNE END
BUCKINGHAMSHIRE

I S B N   0 902875 88 4

Designed and Produced by
Mechanick Exercises, London

Typsetting by Inforum Ltd, Portsmouth
Printed and bound in Great Britain by
Redwood Burn Limited
Trowbridge and Esher

FOR PAULINE

CONTENTS

ILLUSTRATIONS

9

10

ACKNOWLEDGEMENTS

After more than half a lifetime spent in Lancashire, it is impossible to acknowledge the many sources that have helped this book along. How, indeed, to remember whether a particular story lodged in the memory came from a book or newspaper, from family gossip or a chance conversation with one of countless folk the length and breadth of the county?

This is essentially a personal view of Lancashire, a conspectus of a county where a first, and perhaps uncertain, attraction can soon be transformed into a lasting passion. To include every incident of historic worth, every deserving Lancastrian and notable place of interest would require much more than a single volume.

With the exception of Furness, I have taken for my physical boundaries those of pre-1974 Lancashire, when Manchester and Liverpool were embraced by the county limits. These, with their satellite industrial towns, are now counties in their own right, but no tale of Lancashire is complete without them.

Thanks are due to the staffs of the local history libraries in Manchester and Salford; to the publicity offices of Lancashire County Council and the City of Liverpool; and to the editors of the *Lancashire Evening Telegraph* and *Bolton Evening News* for the use of copyright photographs.

Special thanks are due to Bill Lloyd for permission to use material from my *Manchester Evening News* articles, as well as photographs from the paper's picture library.

1 · COUNTY OF CONTRASTS

Look eastward from Rivington Pike and look beyond the great mass of Winter Hill to the open face of the Pennine Fells. Turn to the west to take in the industrial towns, unlovely in close-up but here softened and blurred by distance.

Which is the real Lancashire?

Both are, because Lancashire is a curious and exasperating mixture of rural and industrial England, where town and country live close together in a paradox of friction and harmony.

Stand, for instance, at the centre of Rivington, by the village green and the Queen Anne chapel with its graceful bell-tower, and it is hard to believe that the mills and factories of Bolton are only a handful of miles away. Or walk by the banks of Roddlesworth river, picking your way carefully over the grey stone setts clearly marking the old coaching road from Bolton to Blackburn, and wander undisturbed down to the river, where the banks are still a carpet of bluebells even in mid-June.

But invite a stranger to think of Lancashire, and what springs to his mind? Sprawling cities and worn-out towns, linked in an endless grimy chain of industrial squalor, or perhaps Blackpool's windy, sea-soaked promenade, thronged by holidaymakers escaping from the drab monotonous life of a factory bench or mill loom.

Mental images like these tell part of Lancashire's story, but by no means the whole of it. The commonplace picture of the county, at least for those who view it discreetly from afar, is invariably one of unrelieved gloom. The notion of back-to-back terraces, overhung by a perpetual smoky pall, dies hard. Most of these terraces were bulldozed into rubble years ago and massive clearance schemes are making short work of their counterparts throughout the county.

From the narrow, small-town streets came the workers who created Lancashire's wealth and, at the same time, that of the nation. They produced more than their fair share of men whose genius raised them high above the normal run, whose skill and inventiveness left an abiding mark on the world.

Look at Bolton and you may see only a typical small Lancashire industrial town. Yet it raised Samuel Crompton, who played the fiddle in the theatre orchestra, who wrote his own hymns for the church where he was organist and found enough spare time to invent a machine that turned out fine cotton so cheaply that it gave Lancashire an unbeatable edge over its competitors. The order of priorities in his working life is typically Lancastrian.

Richard Arkwright ran a barber's shop in a Bolton cellar, advertising "Come to the Subterranean Barber, He shaves for a Penny", When his competitors cut their prices accordingly, Arkwright countered with "A Clean Shave for a Halfpenny". He later changed the face of the cotton industry by inventing his water frame spinning machine.

Edwin Chadwick, also of Bolton, built model houses for workers and did more than any man of his day to bring new standards of health and cleanliness to Britain. And Bolton was the birthplace of William Lever, creator of Sunlight Soap and high master of the new art of advertising, who died as Lord Leverhulme and the head of Britain's biggest industrial complex.

To a greater or lesser degree, most of Lancashire's industrial towns can tell an equally impressive story. Probably no other county has played such an important part in the commercial development of the nation, and no other county has bequeathed such a legacy of decay, despoilation and devastation by the Industrial Revolution. Although these scars and half a century of neglect sometimes put faith to the test, Lancashire is undoubtedly one of Britain's most beautiful counties. Take visitors from the south into the open landscapes around Bolton, Preston and Burnley and, after a period of painful disbelief, they are compelled to admit the truth of the claim: the beauty of Lancashire has no equal.

So look at Lancashire as a whole, balancing the outcrops of industry against the surrounding countryside, and paying not too much attention to artificially imposed boundaries that sometimes ignore historic and cultural factors.

Broadly speaking, the county runs south from the lands above the Lune and down to the Mersey, eastwards from the coast to the Pennines, and that, in the view of many Lancastrians, is that, whatever the 1974 boundary revisions may say. Despite the map-makers, Furness was never truly part of Lancashire. Equally, and in spite of Yorkshire claims, the Forest of Bowland and the Trough are essentially part of the western County.

14

Part of the ring of gloomy slums which once encircled Manchester

Away from industry, Lancashire presents three faces to the world, each quite distinct in appearance, history and customs. Together they add up to a landscape of infinite variety and charm, where dialect can change subtly within the space of a few miles and where history stands at every turn of the road.

Embracing both Blackpool and Southport, the flat coastal plain between Morecambe and Liverpool runs west to the motorway, where it gives way to a swell of low foothills and exchanges market gardening for rich dairy farming land. Lancashire's severest face is seen in the fell country and along its Pennine boundary, a largely unpopulated countryside revealing some of its most dramatic scenery.

Rivers draw these three distinct landscapes together. Tranquil waters like the Lune, Wyre, Douglas and Yarrow, or broad rivers of industry like the Mersey and the Ribble. Some, it must be admitted, are doubtful pleasures. Between its source and its junction with the Hodder near the Yorkshire border, the Ribble is sweet and uncontaminated. Once it

15

The Sportsman's Arms at Cliviger, near industrial Burnley

joins the Calder, however, it immediately becomes poisoned. The Calder now carries "highly ferruginous ground " - polluted water finding a natural outlet from an abandoned colliery where the workings are no longer pumped out each day.

The Darwen, the Douglas and Calder pour about 130 million gallons of poisoned water into the Ribble every day. Add the sewage and industrial waste from Preston, and from smallholdings and streams on the way to the river mouth, and it is not surprising that by the time the Ribble reaches the sea its bed is carpeted with a black slime revealed in all its offensiveness at each turn of the tide.

Fish somehow manage to survive in the Ribble and its tributaries, although only a token number compared with the past. In Izaak Walton's days the river Darwen was thick with trout. At Preston, in the mid-eighteenth century, nearly 3,500 salmon and sea trout were caught "all at one draught" from the Ribble. Between 1967 and 1970 the Lancashire River Authority stocked the Leeds and Liverpool canal near Wigan with 676,000 fish. About 50,000 have survived. Chemical analysis shows the water to contain arsenic, lead, zinc and other pollutants,

16

most of them fed into the canal from one river, the Douglas, which two hundred years ago was so clear and pure that it was known as the Lancashire Jordan, because Baptists were immersed in its waters during their baptism rites.

The rivers that flow westward towards the coast are born high on the moors. Hawthornthwaite Fell is the source of the Wyre, while two of its tributaries, the Calder and the Brock, spring from the bleak heights of Bleasdale. On their downward way each river creates its own character, a foaming torrent carving a tortuous way through the rocky slopes, and forming the countryside into its own particular pattern.

Midway between the high fells and the coastal plain the rivers develop in different ways. The Calder thrusts a secret channel through a deep defile, its waters hidden beneath banks of trees unless you seek them out. In contrast, the Brock is broad and slow-moving, winding a gentle course through open country. Its shallow waters are fordable at many points, to the delight of generations of small boys, and its banks are delightful paths through grassy hollows and shady woodlands.

Out in the Fylde the Wyre is master, always widening as it makes its way to the sea as a giant scar across flat farmlands reclaimed from the marshes. At every stage these rivers highlight a particular beauty of the Lancashire landscape. In the fells, it seems, nothing can match their wild grandeur. Later, the lower, green foothills prove equally attractive; and the final quiet splendour of the Fylde, with its promise of the sea, is irresistible.

With such a variety of landscape, history and custom within its borders, it is doubtful whether a typical Lancastrian exists. One may be able to trace one's ancestry back to the seventh-century Anglians, who swept down from the north to settle on the flat lands between the sea and the hills. A neighbour's family may go back to the Mercian invaders, who thrust through the Midlands and across Cheshire. Anglians and Mercians met at the Ribble, a natural boundary of territory and tongue, and on either side of the river, village names still betray their respective origins.

Some Lancastrians may have a dash of Norwegian blood in their veins, for Norsemen sailed up the county's navigable rivers and founded their own settlements, Christian men skilled at farming and fishing.

All these antecedents, and many more, helped to form strong characteristics. Dogged determination, sly deadpan humour, long thoughtful silences and an attachment to legends and superstitions, not to mention an uncanny gift for cutting the pompous or pretentious down to size with a few terse and pointed words - all acknowledge a mixed ancestry.

Most people claim to recognise a Lancashire man almost as soon as

17

they clap eyes on him. Let him open his mouth, they say, and his speech gives him away. In some circles a Lancashire accent is considered a social handicap, probably because it is wrongly associated with a lack of education and common sense. The gormless antics of countless comedians have helped to foster this misguided notion, although it is worth noting that through native wit and shrewdness many a cloth-capped comedian has achieved fame and wealth in exploiting his accent by exaggeration. If anyone should laugh at a Lancashire accent, it is its owner. Often it can be his fortune.

However, there is no such thing as a standard Lancashire accent. There are, instead, a bewildering variety of local accents and dialects, the latter rapidly disappearing in the face of a highly mobile population. Nowadays, it is rare to hear a dialect conversation in Lancashire, although inconspicuous eavesdropping in a remote country district, perhaps on a local bus where all the passengers are 'luv' to the conductor, is sometimes rewarding. Dialect phrases are a different matter and Lancashire talk is still larded with them. Many are simply trenchant comments, often acidly pointed, about someone's character, ambition or activities. Watching a well-dressed businessman, puffed up with his own importance and wealth - the latter probably stemming from the hard graft of his father and grandfather - a Lancastrian will still relish his eventual downfall with the dark comment "From clogs to clogs in three generations".

The enduring idea of the Lancashire man as a cloth-capped, mufflered figure much given to black puddings and hotpot, clogs and bitter beer, is a long way from reality. His standard of living compares favourably with other parts of the country. According to 1973 statistics North Westerners own more washing machines than the national average (71 per cent of households, compared with 67 per cent nationally); nearly a quarter of them own a colour television set; one family in two owns a car and one in twenty own two. At the same time they spend as much on food as the rest of the country, but more than the average on beer and tobacco!

In following the national pattern in its way of living, Lancashire has not avoided the sweeping physical changes and developments common elsewhere. It already has two new towns at Warrington and Skelmersdale, and a third, the Central Lancashire New Town, is proposed around a nucleus formed by Chorley, Preston and Leyland. The New Town Corporation is acquiring vast tracts of land north of Preston for early development, cutting into fine farming land in an area that is still, in part, a quiet rural backwater. The new town will be Britain's biggest, with an estimated population of 420,000 living in 72,000 new homes and

Tarnbrook, a quiet corner on the way to the Trough of Bowland

covering 55 square miles. The scale of the operation is frightening. Grimsargh, a small village between Preston and Longridge, with a population of 1,600, will grow to 52,000 by the end of the century, bigger than the present populations of Leyland and Chorley put together.

Based on 1973 estimates, the new town will cost £900 million. The bill will be met by the taxpayer, and the New Town Corporation sees this "as the most significant way of paying off the debt which the rest of the country owes to Lancashire". The price of being the workshop of the world and making the rest of the country rich in the last century has been a grievous one for Lancashire. Bad housing, pollution, derelict land and the wholesale destruction of natural beauty and pleasant old ways of life were what the North West inherited from the Industrial Revolution.

2 · MANCHESTER, CAPITAL OF THE NORTH

For years Manchester has been nourished on the fat of its past greatness, when it was Lancashire's commercial heart and Britain's second largest city. Despite Liverpool's dubious claims, Manchester is still Lancashire's business centre, but it has dropped well down the big city league table. Birmingham, Leeds, Liverpool and Sheffield have larger populations. Even if the whole of the Greater Manchester area is taken into account, it still takes second place to the West Midlands, with its centre at Birmingham.

Once the fount of ideas that changed the course of world events, Manchester is gripped in a stranglehold of outdated dwellings and factories which are now being cleared and replaced by the city of the future.

Sceptics may scoff when they are told that "what Manchester does today, the rest of the country does tomorrow" but the saying has some foundation in fact. From Manchester came the idea of free trade, the basis of Victorian prosperity. The first canal, the first railway, and the first computer were all built in the city. Even today, moved to London and deprived of its original masthead, the *Guardian* still lives on its Manchester heritage and the profits of its sprightly stablemate, the *Manchester Evening News*.

Manchester's importance goes back to Roman times. As Mancunium it was a major junction linking seven Roman roads. The last traces of Roman greatness are buried beneath the Victorian city, hidden away in railway viaducts and warehouses, and by the canal that cuts across the city centre.

At the time of the 1745 rebellion, a contemporary account describes the city as "the greatest mere village in England, more populous than York or most cities in this kingdom". Twenty thousand people packed its rubbish-laden, smelly and narrow streets, most of them industriously involved in the cotton trade. It was noted for its women's wear "which it has been famous for above a hundred years and has been very much improved of late, by some inventions of dyeing and printing".

The city specialised in other products, "known by the name of Manchester goods, as tickings, checks, hats and all kinds of what they call small wares, such as threads, tapes, filleting, etc., which enrich the town and render the people industrious, resembling those of Holland, the children here being all employed and earn their bread". A print of the time shows the first cotton exchange defined by a central pillar in the open market place.

The city's fine Gothic Collegiate Church was founded anew by Queen Elizabeth in 1578, by the name of Christ's College in Manchester, which foundation was afterwards confirmed by King Charles I in 1636 and incorporated by the same name. An account confirms that Manchester women have also changed little during the centuries. They are "generally very handsome, by which they have acquired the name of Lancashire Witches" - bewitching creatures, that is - "which appellation they really deserve, being very agreeable. But some of the pretty witches choose to distinguish themselves by wearing plaid breast-knots, ribbons and garters tied above the knee, which may be remonstranced as dangerous to the constitution. For that above a lady's knee is of so attracting a quality, it is not only in danger of drawing His Majesty's good subjects in the civil, but military gentlemen off their duty".

By the end of the eighteenth century Manchester was still a sleepy market town, dominated by its medieval church and by Chetham's Hospital School and Library, the oldest *public* library in England. The old Wellington Inn, now carefully preserved on expensive concrete stilts, as part of a modern redevelopment scheme, was only one of more than a score of half-timbered buildings in The Shambles.

Manchester Grammar School was then already nearly three hundred years old. It was founded in 1515 as a free school by Manchester-born Hugh Oldham, Bishop of Exeter, "to occupy children in good learning when they come to an age where they may better know, love, honour and dread God and His laws . . . in this county of Lancashire, where children had pregnant wit but were mostly brought up rudely and idly and not in virtue or cunning or good manners".

Bishop Oldham's rules required boys to attend school at six in the morning, and prohibited cock fighting, the carrying of daggers or other weapons and the assaulting of masters. Militant schoolchildren are not exclusively a late twentieth-century phenomenon. In 1690, enraged by the length of their Christmas holiday, Manchester Grammar School scholars staged a sit-in, seizing control of school buildings and excluding the masters.

Manchester Cathedral

The uprising had a deeper political reason, the majority of boys supporting the Jacobite cause against the Whig sympathies of the High Master. The lads held out for a fortnight, supplied by the people of Manchester with beds, food, firearms and ammunition; the latter the boys used to fire at the legs of their adversaries. Despite the switch to comprehensive education on the part of the city schools, Manchester Grammar School still pursues a steadfast academic course, admitting over 200 boys each year.

By the early nineteenth century, Manchester's population had grown to 187,000 and the market town was poised for the tremendous upheaval that was to turn it into a gigantic, prosperous city. In 1821 an Act of

Chetham's Hospital School; scholars wearing their traditional uniform

Parliament authorised the widening of Market Street, a main thorough-fare described as a "narrow, tortured lane lined with wooded-fronted, irregularly built shops with old fashioned signs in front and tangled gardens behind".

The work occupied twelve years and cost £250,000, an extravagant sum in those days. It was followed by similar work in other main streets, during which Manchester became a borough, then a bishopric and finally, in 1853, a city. Along Market Street a new generation of stores replaced the tiny half-timbered shops, substituting immense plate-glass windows for twinkling bottle-glass panes. A new breed of shopkeeper moved in to match the increasing tempo and fury of trade; thrusting, vigorous men, like William Paulden and David Lewis, who replaced the personal service of the small shop with flamboyant advertising and inge-nious promotions designed to increase turnover and multiply sales.

Their customers came from the vast working-class population attracted to the new factories and setting up home in the freshly developed suburbs of Ancoats and Hulme.

A showman as well as an astute businessman, David Lewis announced the opening of his new store in January 1880 by releasing hundreds of advertising balloons into the sky. Market Street was jammed and the police hurriedly brought up reinforcements to handle the crowds. Neighbouring shopkeepers sued Lewis for causing a public nuisance, but although they won their case they gave the brash newcomer unwitting free publicity that increased his business even more.

By taking one of the new-fangled trams, the public could ride into the city, wander freely about Lewis's store and buy goods available nowhere else outside London. At the same time they could enjoy the latest publicity stunt, like the Venetian week when Lewis flooded the basement and took his customers on a subterranean gondola ride.

William Paulden was another showman. His profits, too, came from young couples setting up home for the first time and needing, among other things, cheap and hard wearing linoleum. Paulden's was the first big store to be lit by electricity and to give free film shows. People came miles for a ride in the electric lifts. The window displays stopped the traffic; live lions, tigers and even elephants prowled behind the plate glass

Chetham's Hospital School; twentieth century extensions
adjoin the old buildings

windows, sometimes with disastrous results. When a young lion escaped, customers mistook it for a large dog, patting and petting it affectionately.

While Paulden and Lewis were making a fortune from working-class families, Thomas Kendal and James Milne were catering for the carriage trade, the factory owners and well-to-do businessmen whose splendid new mansions were springing up in the leafy suburbs of Fallowfield and Withington and even deep in the countryside at Didsbury and Cheadle.

Kendal Milne's was built on the foundations of an already sound business and its owners carefully avoided the publicity of Paulden and Lewis which was considered to be vulgar. From the start they set their sights high and before long they were able to furnish the grand houses of the newly rich from cellar to attic, employing their own cabinet-making workshop and upholstery department as well as their general furnishing store.

To shop at Kendals, "the quality store where quality costs less than you think", was a resounding status symbol. Even a century later, when the family connection had been severed and Harrods were in control, to have a charge account at Kendals was a sign that you had arrived. Its recent history reflects the sweeping social and economic changes that have occurred in Manchester, as elsewhere. A multi-million-pound takeover engulfed Harrods and, in turn, Kendal Milne's. Today the majority of its customers are ordinary folk and the store is indistinguishable from other mass market stores in Manchester or any other large city. Time has also been unkind to the great mansions that housed the wealthy clients. Those nearest the city are either demolished or running to seed as decrepit, tumbledown flats. Only those originally in the country and now in smart built-up commuter areas, are being revived after years of neglect and decay.

Across the road from the Cathedral, the buildings of Chetham's Hospital School are virtually the only link with Manchester's medieval past. In the middle of the seventeenth century, Humphrey Chetham, a wealthy bachelor, bought the property from the Stanley family and founded a school for poor boys. On occasions, the pupils still wear the original uniform of blue coat and yellow stockings, topped by a flat, pancake-style cap. Although Chetham's has always given a good, broadly based general education, it developed its long-standing musical tradition into a choir school for the Cathedral and later into one of the few top-flight junior music schools in Britain. Now it attracts gifted music scholars from all over the country and, as a bonus, struck an early blow for Womens' Lib by admitting girls in 1969.

26

The world's first railway station at Liverpool Road, Manchester

All the world knows that Manchester's prosperity was built on mountains of cotton. The city's first cotton spinning mill was opened by Richard Arkwright in 1780. His water frame was preceded a decade earlier by the revolutionary spinning-jenny, and followed by Crompton's mule and the first power loom. Home based industries gradually withered away as workers were gathered together in the mill. Textile machinery factories mushroomed to equip an ever growing number of mills, and foreign traders established offices and warehouses to ship cheap cotton goods to all parts of the world.

The railway came to Manchester in 1830, usurping canals as the prime and cheapest method of conveying the city's goods throughout Britain and abroad. At the official opening of the first line on 15th September, attended by the Duke of Wellington, Stephenson's *Rocket*

Manchester's tallest building, the CIS tower

St Augustine's Church, built to replace a blitzed Victorian building

managed to kill a Cabinet Minister as it puffed a leisurely way from
Manchester to Liverpool. The opening took place at Manchester's Liverpool Street Station, the oldest railway terminus in the world. It still
stands today, a neglected building in a poor part of the city. It remains
to be seen whether it will survive the proposed redevelopment of the
area.

Wholesale demolition has destroyed much of the city's past, as it did
earlier when Manchester was transformed from a pleasant Georgian
market town into the bustling commercial base of the Industrial Revolution. Nothing now remains of the Cook Street workshop, birthplace of

the first Rolls Royce car, except a commemorative plaque on a wall in Hulme's new concrete jungle.

As a poor Lincolnshire boy, Henry Royce came north in search of fame and fortune. He thought he had found it in making the best cranes and dynamos in his backstreet Manchester workshop, until competitors produced cheaper cranes and dynamos incorporating Royce's original, but unpatented, ideas and improvements. The slump in his business coincided with his disgust at the deafening noise and unreliable design of the Decauville car he drove along the country lanes to his Knutsford home. In spite of the precarious state of his finances, he announced to his startled company secretary that he was going to build three experimental cars.

Who but a hard-headed northerner (even by adoption) would have chosen 1st April as the day on which to launch a new product? On that Friday afternoon in 1904, Hulme's narrow, congested streets resounded to the metallic beat of hammers and spanners wielded by mechanics celebrating the new marvel. Bearing the registration number M612, Royce's car was a paragon among motors. Unlike its noisy, untrustworthy contemporaries, it glided along on a whisper of sound, and careful handmade construction guaranteed its later legendary reliability.

Victorian Manchester was full of builders, intent on transforming the city into a vast workshop and commercial centre. Prosperity not only meant money, but provided boundless confidence that goes hand in hand with limitless resources and constantly overflowing order books. Confidence cries out from the buildings of the time; the immense Portland Street warehouses, grandly stone faced and owing much to the Renaissance palaces of Italian princes; the Free Trade Hall, gutted in the 1940s and since restored; the Bank of England building in King Street, now the offices of a merchant bank; and above all that elaborate monument to civic pride and Victorian values, the Town Hall in Albert Square.

Built to Waterhouse's design, selected from one hundred and thirty competitive entries, the Town Hall took nine years to build and was opened with great pomp and pageantry on 13th September 1877. It symbolised the unshakeable nature of Victorian values, gilded by the immense wealth generated by an ever-increasing volume of trade and guaranteed by native inventiveness, industry and thrift. In these less sure days it is impossible not to marvel at the unyielding confidence expressed in the Great Staircase, reception rooms and Council Chamber of Manchester Town Hall.

The city has its share of interesting churches. The oldest are the Cathedral and the Church of St Ann the first a sombre, oppressive place and

Gateway House, an impressive development leading to Manchester's newest railway station at Piccadilly

the second full of seventeenth-century charm and elegance. The remainder are mostly Victorian. True, St Mary's, Mulberry Street, dates from 1794, but much of the interior work is Victorian. It is generally known as the Hidden Gem, under the impression that it is a jewel of architecture and decoration, but this claim is a matter of widely divergent opinion. The name was coined by Herbert Vaughan, a Victorian Bishop of Salford (and later Cardinal Archbishop of Westminster) who spoke in St Mary's: "No matter on which side of the church you look, you behold a hidden gem." In recent years the church's undistinguished façade has emerged from obscurity following the construction of a new office

31

block in Brazennose Street. Despite its debatable claim to beauty, St Mary's deserves an honoured place in Manchester's history, for this was among the first Catholic chapels to be opened for public worship after the Reformation.

Quite a different matter is the Holy Name Church, a French Gothic extravaganza out of place when it was built in 1869 in the middle of a vast sprawl of working-class houses. These have been demolished, and Hansom's church - he also designed the cab that bears his name - has come into its own amidst the new tower blocks and bridges of a rapidly expanding University. Of the city's modern churches, the most impressive is St Augustine's at All Saints, built to replace its Victorian predecessor destroyed during the 1940 blitz. Designed by Desmond Williams, a talented Manchester architect, St Augustine's combines the intimacy of religious experience with the restrained dignity of modern liturgy. Behind the altar, Robert Brumby's immense ceramic mosaic of Christ in Majesty is an eloquent and moving example of the best in present-day religious art.

The crowning glory of Victorian commercial Manchester is undoubtedly the Ship Canal, thirty five miles of inland waterway linking the sea to the city and ending at Manchester Docks, which are paradoxically sited in neighbouring Salford. The enterprise sprang from the reluctance of Mancunians to rely on the goodwill of Liverpool's dock owners, and an unwillingness to pay ever-increasing dock charges. Liverpool was confident that Manchester could not ship its goods abroad, except through the port, and in a monopoly situation who could stop the dock owners charging as much as they liked for the privilege?

At his Didsbury home in a leafy Manchester suburb, Daniel Adamson decided to break Liverpool's stranglehold. On 27th June 1882, he asked a representative gathering of businessmen to consider "the practicability of constructing a tidal waterway to Manchester and to take such action as may be determined". A simple idea, but one hard to realise, even after a four year examination of the scheme and a recommendation that it was a thoroughly sound commercial undertaking.

From the beginning the plan ran into stiff opposition from Liverpool and from the railway companies. It took three years to pilot the Manchester Ship Canal Bill through Parliament and a further two years to raise the necessary capital and start the work. The actual cost of the canal was double the original estimate of £7 million, and at one stage, only a Manchester Corporation loan of £5 million saved the scheme from being abandoned and gave the Corporation a controlling interest in the Ship Canal Company. To the delight of Mancunians and the chagrin of Liverpool's dock owners, Queen Victoria officially opened the

Holy Name Church, Manchester, a Gothic masterpiece now set in the
heart of the University campus

St Augustine's Church, another view

new waterway on 21st May, 1894. Manchester's Lord Mayor was knighted on the spot and the city was on the way to becoming one of the busiest ports in the realm.

Manchester is again a city of change, and in the confusion it is easy to dismiss it as a city that has lost its way. The vibrant, strident days of the Victorian boom are only a memory and the city has settled for a moderate, not-too-exacting level of commercial enterprise. Its appalling legacy of slums, acre upon acre of dreadful back-to-back housing, is being cleared gradually but not always successfully. The grandiose Hulme redevelopment scheme, hailed by the City Council as the largest and most imaginative rehousing scheme in Europe, stands revealed as a failure.

34

The statue of Gladstone points to the high pinnacled tower of Manchester
Town Hall

When the planners tackled Hulme they forgot the earlier lessons of the pre-war Wythenshawe overspill estate. More importantly, they ignored the fundamental principle that cities are for people, who cannot be bullied, coerced or cajoled into an alien pattern of life. Independent, stubborn and often irrational individuals, prejudiced and unpredictable, they nevertheless want to choose their own way of life and their own pattern of community existence.

Only a few miles from the new Hulme, people still live in their old terraced houses lit by gas and warmed by carefully leaded iron stoves. When electricity was laid on decades ago, several householders chose to stick to gas. Now they are pressing the Corporation to improve their living conditions. "We don't want anyone to think we are complainers", explained one of the occupants, "but we would be grateful if the Corporation could do a bit for us. It would be nice to switch lights on and watch T V". And as a wistful afterthought he added: "We have a mind to keep up with the times."

3 · SALFORD

Without the obliging boundary sign you could walk from Manchester into Salford without being any the wiser. For more than a century Salford has lived in the shadow of its bigger, richer and more elegant neighbour, but its people can be consoled by the fact that way back in history Salford was a flourishing town when Manchester was waiting to be founded.

When Emperor Antoninus Augustus compiled his book of Roman roads in Britain, his itineraries included both Mancunium and Mamucium. Controversy has surrounded these two similar names sited roughly in the same place, but Mancunium is clearly Agricola's fort built at Castle Fields, where the Medlock joins the Irwell, and from which Manchester sprang. Mamucium is probably a latinised form of the Celtic word for mother-town, indicating that a Celtic settlement existed here before the Romans arrived and also the reason for the invaders' Castle Field stronghold.

If this is the case, Salford can claim a longer history than Manchester. Salford's Regent Road, a sad huddle of empty shops awaiting destruction and redevelopment, is the probable line of a Roman road north from Castle Field. After the Roman withdrawal, the lands between the Mersey and the Ribble stood in the front line of the battle for supremacy between Mercia and Northumbria. As a key town, Salford was owned by whoever happened to be the dominant king at the time. Consequently, its citizens enjoyed unusual freedom, being neither slaves nor bondsmen but direct servants of the king.

A royal hall, probably built on a commanding site at a horseshoe bend in the Irwell, must have given the town its name, *soel* (hall) and *ord*(the prince) combining to make Salford. Nearby Pendleton is a corruption of Penulton, "the village beyond the ramparts". In 872 the district fell into the hands of the Danes, the influence of Alfred the Great being restricted to the south. Fifty years later Alfred's son reconquered

Ordsall Hall, Salford

Mercia and set about tackling Northumbria and Cumbria. Salford was again in the firing line, but it survived as a free Saxon borough, virtually self-governing, electing its own officers and prospering through vigorous trade.

The Norman Conquest passed almost unnoticed, northern Lancashire having little attraction for William of Normandy. Salford is mentioned in the Domesday Book as a place with a population of 35,280 and covering 350 square miles. If this seems a great tract to attribute to Salford, it must be remembered that it was the only town of substance in a wide area of woodland, pasture and waste leading to the moors and hill country. It also included Manchester, not important enough to merit an entry of its own.

William gave Salford to one of his earls, Roger de Poictou, who lost it to William Peveril, Lord of Nottingham and the Conqueror's bastard son. Later Salford came into the hands of the Earls of Chester, and it was the Sixth Earl, Ranulph de Blundeirke, who put the town on the map in 1231 by granting it a charter as a free borough. This legalised a situation that had existed in practice for a long time, and Salford's citizens now had the official right of choosing their own Reeve, or Mayor, and their own burghers. They also enjoyed independent jurisdiction in all civil and criminal matters and were guaranteed the right to develop trade and industry unhindered.

There was a penalty clause, however. The charter allowed Salford to serve the king in a wider form, which in practice turned out to be the privilege of providing cash and troops for his military adventures. Because of its status under the charter, Salford also became a refuge. Provided he managed to live there for a year and a day, any man bonded into the service of an outlying lord was automatically emancipated and became a free man.

An odd clause reflected the Earl of Chester's resistance to Papal supremacy, or at least to the increasing interference in national affairs by ecclesiastics, and to the Pope's dominance of the king. Already the Palatinate of Chester, which included Salford, was the only part of the country to escape tithes to Rome. Now Salford's charter forbade the sale of a burgher's rights to the Church: "no burgher to be alienated to religion". Which explains why the city had to wait another four hundred years for a new parish church, and why the centre of religious development shifted to Manchester's collegiate church across the river. If matters had been different, Salford may well have dominated Manchester in the future.

Although Salford's lord and townspeople rejected ecclesiastical meddling in their daily affairs, they certainly held staunch and unswerving religious views. After the reformation most of Salford's main families, like the Radclyffes of Ordsall Hall, held fast to the Catholic faith and suffered accordingly.

When it was built in the fifteenth century, Ordsall Hall was set in a fair landscape of fields and woodlands. Today, much renovated and wearing a rather melancholy look, its sturdy roof and dark walls look out on the docks, a wedge of factories and a Corporation housing estate. How many people living in its shadow know that Ordsall Hall played a part in the Gunpowder Plot? Robert Catesby travelled to the Hall to secure Sir John Radclyffe's support for his murderous mission. Guy Fawkes was also sent to warn Sir John that a warrant was out for his arrest. The house was raided by messengers of the Privy Council, and Guy Fawkes, together with Sir John's daughter, escaped along a secret passageway to Ordsall Ford.

Once out of Ordsall Hall, Guy Fawkes' escape route led along a path past Our Lady's Spring, where for centuries the sick and the crippled, the halt and the lame, had come to bathe in the hope of a cure. Lancashire has its fair share of these allegedly miraculous waters, like those near Tockholes and at Fernyhalgh.

Religious beliefs had altered by the eighteenth century, but the spring was still there. Like Buxton and Matlock in Derbyshire, Salford became, for a brief spell, a fashionable spa. Folk travelled long distances to drink a hopefully restoring glass of spring water. It still bubbles away beneath modern concrete foundations, the only visible sign being a spot on the city map marked Ladywell.

For better or worse Salford shared in Manchester's growth during the Industrial Revolution. At the start of the nineteenth century its population was 18,088; by 1851 it had risen to 85,108. Growth brought with it row upon row of insanitary back-to-back houses and the reputation of being the ugliest, dirtiest and most unhealthy city in Britain. But Salford always had its attractive corners and up towards Eccles the city had its own leafy suburb of splendid Victorian mansions. At one time seven Members of Parliament lived on Eccles Old Road, but their gracious houses and broad gardens have now been replaced by small semis and flats.

As a city with a pre-Roman history, Salford's pride was pricked at being outstripped by its younger neighbour. The colossus on its doorstep was impossible to ignore, although successive Salford Councils acted as though Manchester did not exist, and this attitude resulted in curious anomalies and inconveniences to both sides. Since 1974 the two cities face each other on more equal terms as independent Metropolitan Districts of the Greater Manchester County.

The 'Chapel-bedroom', Ordsall Hall, with the arms of Sir John Radcliffe over the fireplace, and a portrayal of the priests' hiding hole

Although Salford's pride was hurt when Manchester became a city and a bishopric in the nineteenth century, a measure of self respect was restored when William Turner was consecrated the first Bishop of Salford in 1851. True, he was a Roman Catholic Bishop, but Salford always kept strong Catholic links and today Catholics are a substantial proportion of its population.

Dr Turner found his Cathedral incomplete, although the foundation stone had been laid seven years earlier and part of the building had been opened for worship in 1848.

Matthew Hadfield's Gothic building, with a soaring spire, 240 feet tall, was finished five years later. It cost £18,000, a hefty sum in those days, gathered "from the pennies of the poor and the pounds of the well-to-do". Looking at the city then and now, few could quarrel with a nineteenth century opinion that the Cathedral "ranks among the scarce architectural glories of Salford". But the city's filthy, soot-laden air played havoc with the Yorkshire stonework. In the 1950's £30,000 was spent on restoration work, and twenty years later a further £75,000 was spent in the same cause.

Unlike Hadfield's church, the clergy house next door was never completed. For a time successive Bishops of Salford lived there, but in the 1920s Wardley Hall at Worsley became their official residence. Despite being hemmed in by a motorway, a graveyard and two major highways, Wardley Hall is still an exciting place. Built in the reign of Edward VI on the site of a much older house, this half-timbered manor was originally moated, and a great drawbridge controlled entry through a gatehouse to an inner courtyard. The great hall has been spoilt by being split into a number of rooms, and the Hall owes its continued existence to the Earl of Ellesmere who saved it in the nick of time from tumbling down when coal mining weakened the foundations a century or so ago.

For over two hundred years Wardley Hall has been known as the Skull House. Visitors may be unnerved to see a grinning skull looking down at them from a glass case on the stairway wall. There is little doubt that this is the head of Ambrose Barlow, the son of Sir Alexander Barlow of Manchester and a Benedictine monk who served the Worsley area of Lancashire during a time of religious persecution.

On Easter Sunday 1641, Ambrose Barlow was arrested while preaching near Leigh. An armed band of sixty men escorted him to Lancaster, where he was tried, convicted and sentenced to death. On 10th September, aged 55, he was bundled on to a hurdle and dragged through the streets of Lancaster to the place of execution. He was hanged, his body being immediately cut down, butchered into pieces and parboiled in tar. His head was impaled, probably at Manchester, as a grim message which all could readily understand. It was removed secretly by Francis Downes and taken to his home at Wardley, where it was discovered a century later in a box hidden in a ruined part of the building.

The Irwell River has played a major part in the history of both Manchester and Salford. Centuries ago it was the principal source of food for the area, and as they thrust northwards no doubt the Romans bought its salmon, eels and chub from Celts living along the river bank. Although shoals of fish lurked under the Irwell bridges as late as 1820, and private fishing continued for another thirty years, industrial development polluted the river to such an extent that all water life has been virtually extinguished for as long as anyone can remember. Recent years have seen a slight improvement and fish have been spotted close to the docks. Schemes are now afoot to clean up the Irwell and transform its banks into pleasant tree-lined walks.

By doing so, perhaps time may be moved back a hundred years or more, when the river was a playground for both cities. Pleasure boats ferried passengers from Blackfriars Bridge and out beyond the mills and factories into a landscape of open fields. Passengers could disembark at Eccles or Barton and stroll along quiet country lanes for tea at a working farm, returning to the boat for an evening journey back to the city. Or they could cruise along the river to Pomona Gardens, now part of dockland but then covering twenty acres of woodland, orchards and fields, criss-crossed by shaded paths and lanes. Elegant and wealthy ladies from both cities danced the waltz in the splendidly mirrored ballroom; its concert halls were fully booked for music festivals and brass band concerts. Far-fetched as it may appear today, Salford held an annual regatta on the Irwell. According to the *Manchester Guardian* it was an occasion of "bright sunshine and a pleasant breeze, with many flags flying. The river banks were crowded with thousands of spectators, the favoured ones in the enclosure being entertained by the Salford Borough Band".

Tired of water sports, spectators could walk along the river bank to the racecourse, tucked into a loop of the Irwell at Kersal Vale. Races were held here until the 1960s, but horses have now given way to houses and university playing fields. Further along the river at Agecroft, a simple grave marks the last resting place of one of Salford's most unusual citizens, Prince Peter Lobenguela, son of a Matabele King. Pursuing his relentless ambition of a British Africa from the Mediterranean to the Cape, Cecil Rhodes contrived to seize Matabeleland. When the King died in 1894, his son was persuaded to come to England, where he was displayed at fairs and circuses as a rarity, a black savage from Africa. Eventually he settled in Salford where he is still remembered

Wardley Hall; a mid-nineteenth century print

and where until recently, his son worked as a park attendant. There is a certain poignancy in the thought of a Zulu prince resting forever on the banks of the Irwell, the river whose damp mists probably hastened his end.

Satellite towns lie beyond Manchester, once independent and buffered from the cities by tracts of open country. Developing industry quickly nibbled away the fields, until factories, mills and houses became welded together in a seemingly endless urban sprawl that ignored boundaries. Nobody would call this part of Lancashire beautiful, although people living in places like Oldham, Rochdale and Bury share a fierce loyalty to their home town that tolerates no criticism. At times these towns may display an unexpected attractiveness, shining streets, wetly reflecting lamplight or thin sunshine striking through a haze that blurs the sharp edges of shadows, but regrettably the plain fact is that

43

Oldham Town Hall

natural beauty largely disappeared from these parts with the coming of industry.

Lancashire's textile industry was originally based on cottage homes, many sited in the Pennines. By 1550 Manchester was already a key centre for both linen and woollen goods, as well as a market for textiles manufactured elsewhere. Burnley, Rossendale and Bury were largely concerned with wool, and the Long Causeway was the high road for pack horses carrying goods across the hills into Yorkshire. Up on these windswept slopes families scraped a bare living; the man farming the unsympathetic moorland soil and his wife weaving cloth beneath the rafters of their three-storeyed stone house.

Linen manufacture was centred on Preston and Accrington. Blackburn, Bolton and Manchester were noted for fustian, a heavy cloth with a linen warp and a cotton weft. By the late eighteenth century Lancashire had claimed cotton as its own and Yorkshire concentrated on wool, although there was still some overlapping of the two. Rapid developments in textile machinery brought workers together in mills for the first time, but in some places handloom weaving lingered on well into the nineteenth century. The first mills were water-powered, built close to the Rossendale gathering grounds and along the foot of the Pennines, but by 1840 over 80 per cent of mills had switched to steam power and ready access to coal was essential if a mill was to stay in business.

Coal became the vital element in Lancashire textile development. An industry long accustomed to mining small pits - shallow workings that rarely exceeded 100 feet in depth and mined by a handful of men - had to expand rapidly to meet an insatiable demand. By 1860 over ten million tons of coal were being extracted every year in Lancashire. An immense number of tiny pits worked every inch of exposed coal between Liverpool and the Pennines, and the county is still covered with flashes, water-filled depressions caused by the collapse of these shallow excavations. As mining techniques improved, deeper pits were dug like the 1,500 feet Pendleton mine at Salford. One man's working day produced a ton of coal, (not much different from today's productivity figure) worth four shillings at the pithead.

Cheap transport was another key factor. It was provided by waterways, initially along rivers where journey times were slashed by building cuts to eliminate natural loops and bends and new locks helped to regulate the flow of water. Sankey Navigation was the first true canal, built to shift coal from the Haydock mines, followed in 1761 by the first section of the Bridgewater Canal.

The Duke of Bridgewater commissioned James Brindley to build what the waterway experts declared to be an engineering impossibility. His answer was a canal that strode confidently across the landscape, a broad aqueduct spanning roads and streams, high-banked to level out valleys and jumping the Irwell at Barton with a bridge 600 feet long and 36 feet wide, its three great arches one of the wonders of the day. At one end, Brindley's canal penetrated the Worsley collieries, where specially built long, flat-bottomed boats, entered through a small archway and emerged laden with eight tons of coal. In time the colliery waterway system covered 40 miles, a complex web serving four mining levels. At the other end of the canal barges off-loaded their cargo at mills and engineering works lining its banks. Half Manchester's coal was brought to the city by canal, and it was said to have as many waterways within its boundaries as any Dutch city.

The Bridgewater Canal was followed by a string of others linking Lancashire's industrial towns and providing passenger transport as well as cargo facilities. Most 'adventurous of all, a trans-Pennine waterway channelled goods to and fro between Lancashire and Yorkshire, through a complicated system of locks.

Canal supremacy was short-lived. It ended in 1830 on the day the first steam passenger train puffed slowly along the new line from Manchester to Liverpool. If the energy and ambition of the canal builders seems almost unbelievable in these days, that of the railway pioneers is even more confounding. Starting from scratch, in ten years they provided Lancashire with an over-generous network of tracks and stations, drove a rail link across the Pennines to Yorkshire and built an essential section of the line between London and Scotland. Their industry, determination and unbounded confidence was breath-taking.

Consider their record. In 1831 a branch of the Liverpool line arrived at Warrington. The following year another branch was taken to Wigan and two years later, to Preston; links to Lancaster and Carlisle quickly followed. Only seven years after the first commercial railway was opened, Birmingham was connected to Warrington via Crewe and you could travel by train all the way from Manchester to London. Crossing the Pennines the railway builders faced the same problems so successfully overcome by the canal promotors fifty years earlier. A line through Rochdale and along the Calder Valley to Hebden Bridge, then via the Aire Valley to Leeds, was completed by 1841. Three years later the way to Sheffield was open, an enterprise that involved cutting three miles of tunnel through the Pennines at Woodhead.

In modern terms, a comparable effort would be the creation of a comprehensive motorway network in the space of a decade. In fact it has taken us a quarter of a century to build the *beginning* of a motorway system.

By 1850, in contrast, Lancashire not only had railway links with every major industrial centre, but also lines connected to its own towns and intermediate villages. It had become the most urbanised part of Britain, the principal industrial region of the nation and of the world. Its urban population had increased fourfold, rising from 300,000 town dwellers in 1801 to 1,200,000 at the time of the 1851 Census. This same period saw Lancashire divided into areas of textile specialisation, with weaving in Blackburn and Burnley, and spinning in Rochdale and Oldham. Manchester was principally a spinning centre, although most of the mills combined both activities. Lancashire dominated the textile scene, controlling nearly 65 per cent of an industry that provided over half of Britain's export income. Textiles created 170,000 jobs in the county, apart from countless others in the allied trades of engineering, chemicals and coal mining.

Such unprecedented industrial expansion altered the landscape out

Bury, the birthplace of Sir Robert Peel

of all recognition. Once quiet, almost isolated villages, became flourishing towns firmly wedded to an industrial belt with Manchester as its centre. In 1750 Oldham was a village of less than a hundred houses. A century later it had a population of over 72,000, the majority working in the mills and living in steep terraces that remorselessly ate deep into moorland slopes. Natives call it *Owdham*, regret the passing of duck and muffins and are proud it was the birthplace of a great British composer, Sir William Walton.

In Oldham, as elsewhere in this area of Lancashire, you may still hear the cry "Oh, go to Jericho!", the final phrase in an exchange that has left the speaker choked with irritation at another's vexatious importunity. But to find Jericho you must go to nearby Bury, the home of the black pudding and birthplace of Robert Peel.

47

The clock tower, Bury

Probably few people in Bury associate the bobby on the beat with one of their own townspeople. Sir Robert's first policemen were affectionately called peelers, and later bobbies. Both his grandfather and father made fortunes from textiles and, securely bolstered by immense wealth, Robert Peel entered Parliament at the age of twenty-two. Throughout his life he held fast to his principles, whatever the cost. As Prime Minister he defied all opposition and levied a tax on incomes above £150 a year. Within three years his Income Tax had wiped out a Budget deficit of £2 million and provided a useful surplus of £5 million.

Peel enraged traditionalists by supporting Catholic emancipation. Faced with a hungry and ever-increasing population he repealed the laws that imposed taxes on imported foodstuffs, ending the centuries old protection enjoyed by British farmers. Gentry and big business hated Peel, but to the mass of the population he was a hero. After a defeat in the Commons he spoke his own epitaph: "I shall leave a name execrated, I know, by every monopolist. But it may well be that I shall be sometimes remembered with expressions of goodwill in those places which are the abodes of men whose lot it is to labour and earn their daily bread by the sweat of their brow. In such places, perhaps, my name may be remembered with expressions of goodwill when they who inhabit them recruit their exhausted strength with abundant and untaxed food, the sweeter because it is no longer leavened with the sense of injustice".

The Pennines breathe down Rochdale's neck, their bracing winds scouring the streets and sending the unwary back for a thicker overcoat. The dour hills and their arduous climate must be responsible, at least in part, for the streak of determination that runs through the Rochdale character as thoroughly as the word Blackpool in a stick of rock. John Bright was born here in 1811, a Quaker described as the "greatest orator that this generation has seen". Together with Robert Peel and Richard Cobden, Bright worked ceaselessly for the repeal of the Corn Laws and the promotion of Free Trade.

In the winter of 1844 a group of working men gathered together in a tiny brick shop in a Rochdale street. At a time when most working families were either starving or living at a pitifully low level of subsistence, these men - they called themselves Pioneers - each subscribed £1 and opened the first Co-operative. Their rules of business were simple; pure and unadulterated goods sold at a fair price for ready cash, and each shareholder to have one vote whatever the size of his investment or the amount of goods bought. Shares carried a fixed interest, and any extra profits were shared out as dividends between members according to the extent of their purchases.

From these simple notions emerged the Rochdale Pioneers Co-opera-

Rochdale, the old and the new. Modern high rise flats contrast with
nineteenth-century terraces

tive Society, the forerunner of similar societies in virtually every major
town in the country. Until the last war the movement was a way of life
for thousands of housewives, characterised by an almost religious fervour and a mystical attachment to the 'divi'.

Between the wars Rochdale set another example in co-operation,
tackling its unemployment problems by putting men to work demolish-
ing the worn-out town centre and creating a new boulevard and gardens. Thanks to this far-sighted arrangement, open spaces now surround
the town hall, one of the finest in Lancashire. The clock tower has an elegance that puts Big Ben to shame and the building happily avoids the
clumsiness often associated with Victorian public monuments. At the
top of the richly carved staircase, the medieval-style Council Chamber
has a stout hammerbeam roof resting on sixteen angels, a joyous extrav-
agance that reflects the Rochdale conviction that nothing is too good
for this town.

4·IN THE SHADOW OF
WINTER HILL

Nearly 1,500 feet above sea level and only a few miles north of Bolton, the summit of Winter Hill must be one of the loneliest and least hospitable spots in Lancashire. On a clear day it is an unsurpassed vantage point, from which the greater part of the county may be seen with pin-sharp definition. Under particularly good conditions the Pennine spine can be followed from Pen-y-ghent in Yorkshire's Craven country down to Derbyshire's giant peaks. Looking south, the Welsh mountains stand out sharply, with Snowdon's massive crest thrusting through wispy cloud.

For all its remote bleakness, Winter Hill has seen a great deal of human activity. Prehistoric man certainly lived here and burial mounds by the summit are reckoned to be over 3,500 years old. Until the last century, coal, iron and lead were mined on the surrounding moors; their hollows and clefts became quarries for slate and stone.

Near the top of Winter Hill, Scotsman's Stump recalls a particularly brutal murder. A plate fixed to a cast-iron pillar tells of "George Henderson, traveller, native of Arran, Dumfriesshire, who was barbarously murdered on Rivington Moor at noonday, 9th November, 1838". The twenty-year-old victim worked for a Blackburn drapery firm and was discovered dying on a moorland track crying "I am robbed, I am killed". On scanty evidence, a Horwich man called Whittle was accused of the murder, but at his trial the jury returned a 'Not Guilty' verdict.

Rivington village lies at the foot of the moors, and the best approach is through a pair of polished granite pillars at the northern end of Horwich. The pillars mark the entrance to Lever Park, a gift to the people of Bolton from William Lever, a noted Rivington landowner whose fortune was based firmly on Sunlight Soap. Before the park was made, the wide sweep of road was only a rough footpath and the new road joins a much older one on the way to the village.

Although Lever's park was intended for "the benefit of the citizens of

51

Rivington Pike and Tower seen from the lowlands of the coastal plain

his native town and neighbourhood", surprisingly its ownership and care are vested in the city of Liverpool, a fact that conceals a story of intrigue, petty jealousies and cut-throat negotiation.

William Lever bought the Rivington estates at the end of the nine-teenth century and set about building a splendid bungalow on a rough, high ridge not far from Rivington Pike. New roads were made to serve the cottage, and the place included four lodges, a garage and workshop, stables and an elaborate pigeon tower.

On 6th September 1901, Lever instructed his agent to offer part of his Rivington lands to Bolton Corporation as a gift "for free and uninter-rupted enjoyment by the public", retaining the right to provide, at his own expense, whatever buildings, roads and paths he judged necessary for the proper opening up of the land for public enjoyment. Bolton Cor-poration gratefully accepted his offer the following December, but the city of Liverpool threw a massive spanner in the works.

Alarmed that Lever's new public park would harm their important water supplies drawn from Rivington reservoirs, Liverpool gave notice of a Parliamentary Bill for the compulsory purchase of Rivington parish, including church, chapel and grammar school. Bolton objected and a Parliamentary committee eventually found an acceptable compromise. Lever's park could go forward, but the land must be vested in the City of Liverpool, who must then maintain it for the use of the Bolton people.

Although Rivington village and its buildings were excluded from the final Bill, William Lever's other lands near the reservoir did not escape compulsory purchase. Liverpool Corporation offered £40,000 for them; Lever demanded £457,000. Arbitration followed, conducted by eminent (and expensive) Counsel on both sides. In evidence it was said that improvements to Lever's Rivington estates had already cost over £130,000. The arbitrators awarded him £138,499, but in the end he had to take Liverpool Corporation to Court to get his money. By today's standards the amounts quoted are considerable; by 1902 values they were astronomic.

The completion of the park, including an open air zoo, a boating lake and a copy of the ruins of Liverpool Castle, was celebrated by a luncheon at Rivington Hall on 10th October 1911. Sir William Lever, as he had become by then, had a field day, proposing five out of the seven toasts. Two years later his public generosity was ill-rewarded when Suffragettes set his bungalow ablaze. The timber building and its collection of valuable pictures was totally destroyed. Undeterred, Sir William had the site cleared and built a new bungalow at a cost of £30,000, this time using stone and concrete.

By 1920 the total expenditure on Lever's new Rivington home and estate had reached £250,000. The gardens must have accounted for a large slice of this money, for no expense was spared in transforming harsh, unsympathetic moorland into an elegant series of terraces. Massed rhododendrons, azaleas and honeysuckle contrasted with fir trees and moorland heather. Alpine plants covered miles of stepped paths between terraces and courtyards; streams and waterfalls gushed and cascaded through fresh woodlands.

Liverpool Corporation had its eventual revenge. After the death of Viscount Leverhulme the Corporation bought the Rivington property. In 1947 the bungalow was demolished and the gardens abandoned. Now only one or two patches of chequered floor tiling and a few tumbled stones remain of this once splendid building, although the workshop and the pigeon tower still stand near the lodge gateways. Nature quickly reclaimed the gardens, but recently enthusiasts have been hacking away at the creeper growth strangling the terraces and it is now possible to recapture some idea of what the gardens must have been like in their hey-day.

Thieve's Grave lies along the Rivington road, recalling a legend from Norman times when Rivington's Lord of the Manor hunted in Horwich Forest and was plagued by poachers. Local people saw no reason why venison and game should be reserved exclusively for his table, and made free use of his lands. The Lord of the Manor caught one of the poachers red-handed and hung him from a tall oak, leaving the body to swing as a grim warning to others.

In retaliation the poacher's comrades burst into the Manor House, killing the Lord's wife and hanging his three children from the same tree that still bore their colleague, and later burying the tiny bodies in an unknown grave. From then on, runs the tale, every night their ghosts wandered restlessly about Rivington. Terrified inhabitants called in the local priest, who conducted a service where the children were thought to be buried and the alarming ghostly activities ceased. The murderers were themselves captured and suspended from the same oak.

Great House Farm and Barn stand on the left of the road as it nears the village, opposite a broad drive leading to Rivington Hall. The oldest part of the farm dates from the seventeenth century, but the adjoining barn, now a refreshment room for visitors, has a much longer history. True, its stonework was restored at the turn of the present century, but its massive oak frame, like an upturned Viking boat, may go back as far as the ninth century. A nearby cottage was once the home of Philip Gibbs, who lived here in the early 1900s and paid two shillings a week rent. Every morning the future knight left his wife and child to walk down to Horwich for the tram to Bolton, where he worked as a journalist on a local paper.

Rivington Hall was once the centre of village life, the home of the thane in Saxon times and in medieval days the Lord of the Manor's house. The last of these sold the Manor to William Lever less than a hundred years ago. The original fifteenth-century half-timbered and plastered house was replaced by the present Georgian building in mellow brick, both built by the Pilkington family, Lords of the Manor since the mid-1400s.

A pleasant Green marks the centre of Rivington, overlooked by the schoolmaster's house, a post office and an elegant Queen Anne chapel. The land for the chapel, Lancashire's first Nonconformist place of worship, was bought in 1703 for fifty shillings. Inside, a stone memorial records the ejection of the minister from Rivington church: "Ye Revd. Samuel Newtone, driven from ye Church on Bartholomew Sunday 1662".

Tockholes; once a centre of dissent and illegal distilling

Earlier, the vicar of Rivington had been one of 2,000 Anglican clergy-men expelled from their livings because they would not accept forms of worship ordained by the Puritan authorities. During the following fif-teen years, Rivington had four Puritan ministers, but the restoration of the monarchy was quickly followed by the Act of Uniformity and a return to an episcopal Church of England and the Book of Common Prayer.

Now the boot was on the other foot, and clergymen who refused to conform were kicked out. Samuel Newton was one of sixty-seven Lan-cashire ministers who stuck fast to Nonconformism and lost their churches. They continued preaching, their followers meeting in secret in isolated barns or lonely moorland dells until the laws were relaxed sufficiently to allow them to build their own chapels.

A few yards from Rivington Green, at a lower level, is one of Lanca-shire's most historic schools. The uncompromisingly Edwardian struc-ture is a remodelled eighteenth-century school, itself built on the site of the original Free Grammar School of Queen Elizabeth, established in 1566. Its enlightened founder was James Pilkington, a native of Riving-ton and one of Elizabeth's new bishops. A staunch supporter of the new Church of England, he had a hand in drawing up the revised Prayer

Book and was rewarded by the see of Durham in 1561. Eight years later he fled from his Cathedral disguised as a beggar in the face of Catholic uprisings, but not before he had provided his Rivington Grammar School with a set of rules that would probably bring any present day student out on strike. In spite of the bitter winters, the boys rose at 5.30 a.m. Classes lasted from six in the morning until six in the evening, all lessons and conversation being in Latin. This rigorous day still left them with enough spirit and energy for boyish high jinks, including some that may appear rather advanced to modern eyes. The rules laid down the punishment for boys found in ale houses or fighting in the streets, and also for what is quaintly described as "haunting houses". The old grammar school building is now used as the village primary school, surely one of the most beautifully sited in Britain. Local opinion has managed to keep the school open, despite the education authority's antipathy towards small rural schools.

On the Belmont Road the fingerpost points along an unmade lane to Rivington Pike, whose history goes back much farther than the time when the stumpy stone tower was built on its crest. From the twelfth century it was one in a long chain of beacons, fiery alarm signals alerting the countryside in times of danger. At the beginning of July, 1588, orders were given for Rivington beacon to be made ready in case the Spanish Armada was sighted in the Channel. It was fired once, on 19th July, but a day and night watch was kept for eighty-two days at a total cost of £17 1s. 6d. Early in the nineteenth century stocks of wood were again assembled on the Pike ready to give warning of a French invasion.

The now ruined tower was built in 1733 to celebrate the union of Rivington Manor once again, after being split between two owners for more than a century. Because much of the stonework was filched from the base of the old beacon the tower cost a modest £85, and for a long time was used as a shooting lodge for guests at Rivington Hall.

The metalled road near the Pike runs across the fells and down to Belmont, where it crosses the main Bolton to Blackburn highway in a dip. Trapped between these two towns, a wild and tough landscape has stoutly resisted change, whether from Romans building their roads northwards or from the industrial towns of the last century.

The fell people remained a race apart, hard-working, hard-headed but far from hard-hearted once a stranger had gained their respect and approval. Most of them lived in farms and cottages already old when the new-fangled canals and railways brought mills and factories almost to their doorsteps. Only twenty years ago these fells were still remote and unpeopled, the villages little more than a line of cottages on either

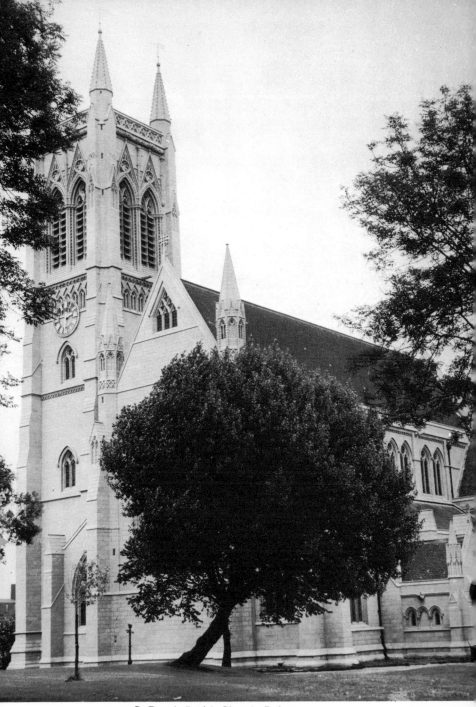

St Peter's Parish Church, Bolton

side of a quiet lane. Then you could have your pick of empty dwellings, abandoned to the mercy of time and weather. All that has changed. Twenty-five years of prosperity, at least for the majority of people, have left their mark on the countryside. The urban noose is tightening around the neck of the fells and new industries from the towns lap against the open fields. New housing estates nibble into the lower slopes of the moor and spindly pylons stride across the fell like some science fiction nightmare. Urbanisation moves on apace, and old farms and cottages that come on the market are snapped up at skyhigh prices for restoration as commuter homes. Fortunately, a great deal of unspoilt country remains and a touch of prosperity has given many a seventeenth-century working farmhouse a fresh coat of paint and an unusual trimness.

Before the new Belmont Road was built, the way from Bolton to Blackburn followed a different line along the course of the Hoddlesworth river. You can still stroll along this old pack road, stumbling over giant setts dislodged by rainstorms and lack of maintenance. Although the sound of traffic is carried faintly from the distant main road, the old highway is a tranquil backwater, impassable for cars and used only by a few walkers and children from neighbouring farms.

Only a few stony foundations remain of the old cottages that used to line this steeply sloping lane down to the river. Like the road, they were abandoned, and their stones carted away for newer houses in nearby Tockholes. This, too, was the fate of Hollinshead Hall, home of the Hollinshead family until the last century. The Hall was used as a farm until fifty years or so ago, but now it is nothing more than a few tumbled stones and leaning doorposts more than half-hidden beneath a tangled mass of vegetation. But the medieval holy well is still there, gushing from a lion's mouth in a tiny chapel known to thousands of pilgrims in the Middle Ages.

Tockholes stands in a dip in the fells, along a horseshoe side lane off the main road. Tucked away in a tree-shaded churchyard, the old schoolhouse has an unusual outdoor pulpit used for open air services during the summer. Because of its isolation Tockholes was a centre of dissent. It was also a centre of illicit spirit distilling. Probably no other village of its size has so many chapels, all set up soon after Charles II's Act of Indulgence in 1672. Even then the Nonconformists had to tread warily, as they soon learned. Judge Jeffreys showed them the letter of the law, rather than its spirit, when he visited the North in 1678.

A grave in Tockholes churchyard marks the last resting place of John Osbaldeston, and its simple inscription records his invention, the weft fork, an indispensable device that stops a loom immediately a thread breaks. Towards the end of his life, Osbaldeston wrote his own epitaph, but no one had the courage to carve it on his memorial:

Here Lies
J O H N   O S B A L D E S T O N
a Humble Inventor
who raised many to Wealth and Fortune
but Himself lived in Poverty and Died in Obscurity
a Dupe of False Friends
and the
Victim of Misplaced Confidence

These bitter words tell nothing but the truth. Although unlettered, John Osbaldeston was a natural genius whose fertile mind produced a string of inventions that improved textile manufacture. He should have become one of Lancashire's richest men, but he died penniless in the local workhouse. Drink and his companions were his worst enemies. The two conspired against him at the inn, where plied with ale he talked freely about his ideas. Between buying the next round, his companions made a careful note of his thoughts, later putting them into practice and patenting the result in their own names.

Eastward from Tockholes the fells continue across the Darwen road to the Forest of Rossendale - there are precious few trees now - and on to the Pennines. A Roman road runs parallel with the main Darwen to Bolton highway, cutting through Edgworth and Blacksnape. It runs, arrow-straight, up and over the hillsides, ignoring natural contours in its eagerness to reach the Ribble. Here the Romans built their Ribchester fort, keeping river pirates at bay and guarding their lines of communication with Hadrian's great wall for over three hundred years.

Bolton is at the base of this wide spread of fell country. The town's importance and prosperity have always rested firmly on textiles. In the twelfth century it was a great woollen town, a regular port of call for Flemish weavers. By the eighteenth century Bolton was busy spinning yarn and handloom weaving, setting the scene for the burst of cotton prosperity a hundred years later.

Bolton's reputation for fine cotton-spinning rested not only on the quality of its goods but on four Lancashire men, all born within a fifty-year span, who invented machines that made it all possible. John Kay was born near Bury in 1704. He had an agile mind and invented the flying shuttle, the abrupt catapult action of which eliminated throwing the shuttle by hand from one side of the loom to the other. Only a leather thong stopped its rapid travel and prevented it smacking the eye of the passer-by. Kay's invention was the start of new methods that spelt the end of home industries and foreshadowed the mills of the future.

Next came a poor weaver, James Hargreaves, born in Blackburn in 1745. Although Kay's shuttle had speeded up weaving, the spinning side of the business was still done at home on antiquated hand wheels. Young Jenny Hargreaves knocked over her mother's spinning wheel, and her father saw that it continued to revolve even when the spindle was upright. If it could drive one wheel in this position it could drive more, and he quickly knocked up a machine with eight spindles.

With one machine doing the work of eight women, a seller's market in yarn quickly became a buyer's free-for-all. Wedded to their hand wheels, angry cottage spinners drove Hargreaves out of Lancashire, but not before he had sold some of his machines, now called *jennies* after the daughter who started the whole affair. These sales were his undoing, for although he later patented his invention, the rights were successfully challenged because the machines were in commercial use before the patents had been granted. Hargreaves did not die in poverty, but he never received the rewards that were his due.

Richard Arkwright was a native of Preston, born in 1732. He spent some years as a Bolton barber, but his natural aptitude for invention went hand in hand with unusually keen financial and business skills. He tinkered with textile machinery and using his natural gift for mechanics developed an existing roller spinning machine into a water frame. To avoid gangs who roamed Lancashire smashing new textile machinery, Arkwright took his water frame to Nottingham. There he gathered his workers under one roof, and Nottingham's first mill was quickly followed by many more in Lancashire. A new way of life, which proved a very mixed blessing, was born. Arkwright was duly knighted and ended his days a very wealthy man.

Hall-i'-th'-Wood, Bolton, a Tudor house once the home of Samuel Crompton

Smithills Hall, Bolton

The last of these four men was Samuel Crompton, a Bolton lad who lived at Hall-i'-th'-Wood, a Tudor mansion fallen on less splendid days. His father died shortly after Samuel's birth in 1753, and his mother earned a meagre living from home spinning and handloom weaving. For spinning they used one of Hargreaves' early jennies, which was a constant source of trouble. Although both the spinning-jenny and Arkwright's frame produced threads strong enough for the weft (the thread that runs the width of the cloth), those for the warp (along the length of the cloth), were either too weak or too coarse.

Crompton patiently experimented and after five years perfected a machine that produced thread as fine as the finest Indian muslins; Lancashire's ascendancy of the cotton trade was now guaranteed. Because it was a hybrid machine, a cross between those of Hargreaves and Arkwright, it was called Crompton's mule. The inventor was now at the mercy of cut-throat businessmen. He had no money to patent his machine, and although he did his best to protect his invention by screening the windows at Hall-i'-th'Wood, it was clear that his secret could not be kept for long.

Eventually Crompton agreed to let a group of cotton manufacturers use his machine in return for a suitable fee. Immense sums were promised, but once the secrets of the mule were known he received the beggarly sum of £68. While cotton manufacturers waxed fat from the profits created by Crompton's mule, its inventor had hardly a penny to his name. In 1809, hearing that a power loom inventor had received £10,000 from a grateful Government, Crompton decided to try his luck

61

in that direction. At last his fortunes seemed to take a turn for the better. The Prime Minister thought £20,000 a reasonable sum, and other Ministers agreed. But on the night when the proposal was to be formally debated in the House, the Prime Minister was assassinated. His successor was less generous, and Samuel Crompton finally received £5,000, which he lost through poor investment. At the end of his life he lived on an annuity of £63, barely twenty-four shillings a week, subscribed by a few loyal friends.

In Crompton's day Hall-i'-th'Wood was set in pleasant wooded fields. The oldest part was built of wood and plaster by the Brownlow family in the fifteenth century, and the same family extended the place a century later. When the Brownlow fortunes crumbled the house was bought by Christopher Norris, a Bolton cloth merchant. His Puritan son, disposing of confiscated Royalist estates, was soon wealthy enough to demolish much of the Hall and rebuild the stone mansion with the mullioned windows we see today.

The Hall came into the Starkey family in 1655 as part of a marriage settlement, but a hundred years later it was let off in tenements, one of which was occupied by the Cromptons. Finally, Hall-i'-th'-Wood fell into disrepair, until Viscount Leverhulme bought the place, thoroughly restored it and presented it to his native town. The once open meadows are now filled with houses and factories, but the Hall remains and is open to the public as a legacy from the past, splendidly furnished as the home of a fairly wealthy family of Tudor times.

Hall-i'-th'-Wood looks across Bolton at another ancient house built on the slopes of Smithills Moor and also owned by the town. When it was built before the fourteenth century, the first owners of Smithills Hall were the Knights Hospitallers. It has grown piece by piece over the centuries, and although much of it is now overlaid by Victorian alterations, the fourteenth-century Great Hall remains virtually intact, an immense space with a soaring roof and giant timbers.

The sixteenth-century drawing-room still has its oak beam ceiling and its original linenfold panelled walls. A curious indentation in the floor of the corridor leading to the chapel is carefully protected. This, legend would have one believe, is the footprint of George Marsh, examined and condemned at Smithills as a heretic. After interrogation and sentence he is said to have stamped his foot on the stone flags as proof of his faith and his cause, leaving a deep and permanent indentation on the stone. This striking example of his innocence cut no ice with his captors; he was tied to a stake and burnt to death.

5 · LIVERPOOL TO SOUTHPORT AND WIGAN

Sometimes good-hearted, sometimes viciously cut-throat, the long-standing rivalry between Liverpool and Manchester makes it tempting to write in comparative terms about the two cities. This would be an injustice to both, for each has its own identity and its own place in Lancashire's story. Manchester is rooted at the centre of the county's affairs; Liverpool, on the other hand, looks farther afield.

If its claim to be the capital of Lancashire is disputed, Liverpool can, oddly enough, make fair claim to be the principal city of North Wales. Even its name betrays Welsh origins, *Lle'rpwll*, the place of the pool, being progressively anglicised through *Lyrpwil* to Liverpool. Its earliest shipping routes were to Anglesey and the Welsh coastal ports. When Henry VIII made over the city's taxes to its mayor for £14 a year, the lease refers to the seaport as *Lyrpal* and names the mayor as David ap Gruffyd. As late as the end of the eighteenth century, the city circulated its own Welsh penny. As a major port, Lancashire's western terminus, Liverpool's eye, ranges across all quarters of the world.

The price of isolation from the centre of affairs is balanced by the profitable advantage of being the main place of passage for people and goods to and from the county. It is a multi-national city, less so now than a century ago, when Welsh, Scots and Irish lived there in large numbers, mingling happily with a sizeable Chinese community and settlements of immigrant Jews from Spain, Poland, Germany and Russia.

Set against a background of easy-going Lancashire tolerance, for a time Liverpool was a well-integrated city, where citizens of many nationalities worked together in cordial harmony, yet remained free to follow their own customs and beliefs. In the eighteenth century, John Wesley was able to point approvingly at Liverpool's tolerance of minorities. Fifty years later, when the city became a refuge for Irish escaping famine, and the harsh repression of English landlords and an English army, he would have spoken in contrary terms.

For many Irish refugees, Liverpool was merely a staging post to the United States, but thousands of others remained in the city to provide a pool of cheap and expendable labour. Through force of circumstance, the majority of those who stayed nevèr improved their lot, living in appalling conditions, seeking oblivion in countless seedy pubs in the city centre and readily lending their voices and fists to fiery political and religious causes.

A few prospered, and prospered rapidly, acquiring envied positions in Liverpool society and politics, dragging into the public area the confrontation that earlier had been confined to the three ale bar. For a century or more, hatred between sects and factions became a sad, but indisputable, feature of Liverpool life.

At the time of the Norman Conquest, Liverpool was so unimportant that the lordship of the manor was exchanged for a pair of falcons. It made little headway for two hundred years, until King John needed a northern port to replace Chester, then under the iron control of one of his northern earls. Liverpool's first Royal Charter of 1207 did little more than make it a staging post for small inshore craft, and larger vessels sailing to Ireland and the Isle of Man. The town struggled on for

Liverpool's imposing waterfront. From left to right, the Liver Building, the Cunard Building and the Dock Offices

another five hundred years, dreaming perhaps of a greatness that lay within its grasp but somehow achievement, when it did arrive, was borne on the blood and misery of African slaves.

Slavery was nothing new. Hawkin's successful voyage in Queen Elizabeth's own vessel started the profitable London trade, many of whose merchants in human cargo moved to Liverpool in the seventeenth century to escape the plague. The northern port began to trade with the newly established settlements on the other side of the Atlantic, exchanging poor and ignorant Englishmen and women for tobacco from the Americas.

Consciences were never easy when shipping white men as slaves from Britain. African negroes were a different proposition, a trade in which a gentleman could engage without compunction. Gradually Liverpool vessels established a regular triangular course, outward to Africa, exchanging manufactured goods for slaves, then from Africa across the Atlantic to America, where the human cargo was bartered for tobacco and rum for the homeward voyage. In an amazingly short time Liverpool dominated the trade, its 105 slave ships carrying nearly half the world's annual traffic in pitiable living flesh.

Of the millions of slaves shipped across the Atlantic, each curly head worth £1 clear profit, about a third survived. Aboard ship they lay side by side like sardines in a can, each chained hand and foot to his neighbour and occupying no more than eighteen inches of deck space.

Conditions on slave ships were intolerable, immeasurably worse than those on Royal Navy vessels, generally recognised at the time as being scarcely endurable. To find their crews, slaver captains were forced to resort to all kinds of trickery and deceit. Once at sea, they had to transform an unwilling rabble into gunners capable of fending off attacks from marauding French privateers and strong-arm men quick to quell any revolt by newly loaded slaves, still vigorous enough at the start of a voyage to put up a fight. Crossing the Atlantic, crewmen battled against typhus, dysentery and scurvy engendered by crowded mess decks and packed holds. No wonder that common humanity was soon forgotten and the simplest way of dealing with sickness or revolt was to throw the offending negro overboard.

Liverpool's willing share in this inhuman trade was partly offset by the efforts of some of its citizens to put a stop to it. The Society for the Abolition of the Slave Trade was formed in the city in 1787, and men like William Rathbone and William Roscoe earned the contempt, and more, of Liverpool merchants by raising a national outcry against the trade.

When slavery was finally outlawed in the early nineteenth century,

Liverpool's wealth was already made. The problem was how to guarantee its continuance. Ironically, the solution was found in the very cotton plantations worked by slaves shipped to America in Liverpool vessels.

Britain's first cotton auction was held in Liverpool in 1757. Trade in cotton grew alongside trade in slaves, raw cotton joining tobacco and molasses on the homeward passage from America. On Liverpool Flags, the open-air cotton market that preceded the building of the city's imposing trading exchange, top-hatted and frock-coated merchants haggled and bargained, their air of assurance sometimes concealing a gnawing anxiety as to whether their gamble on a price twelve months earlier would pay off now that their cotton-laden ship from America had been sighted off Hoylake.

In the early days of cotton, advance knowledge of a vessel's arrival often meant the difference between a fat profit and a crippling loss. Lancashire cotton men devised ingenious schemes to be the first with the

Liverpool's Cotton Exchange

news of an arrival; one enterprising merchant paid horsemen to relay the sighting of cotton ships off Anglesey back to his Liverpool home.

Changes came hard on the heels of cotton prosperity. Canals slashed transportation costs, ending the monopoly of turnpike roads that had never been suitable or convenient for the transport of merchandise. In turn, waterways gave way to railways, and both Manchester and Liverpool claim the distinction of being responsible for this new mode of transport. As the first railway ran between the two cities, the claim will never be resolved to the satisfaction of both parties, but Liverpool's other railway, an elevated electric system through dockland now replaced by a motor road, was the first of its kind in the world. Its underground railway, competing with the Mersey ferries, preceded the famous road tunnel by almost half a century.

Ships and docks play a large part in Liverpool's story, despite its hazardous approach by sea. The Mersey is not the easiest of rivers to

Liverpool Docks in its heyday, with overhead railway (now demolished)

navigate, nor is it the happiest entry to a labyrinth of docks and warehouses. Scouring sands and a vigorous tide race are ever-present hazards, and up to the end of the seventeenth century boats anchored under the protective lee of Liverpool Castle, the ebb tide leaving them high and dry on tilted keels.

Overcoming early problems of silting, Liverpool's first dock was the forerunner of an extensive network of port facilities. For the first time it brought ships close to the city centre, and contemporary prints show slender tall masts joining church spires to create a sky pattern above a terraced townscape.

Quality of design and workmanship characterised the great expansion of Liverpool docks in the nineteenth century. Whether built in brick, stone or cast iron, or a combination of all three, the quays, warehouses and offices were remarkable architectural achievements. Even the dockland furniture, bollards, capstans, handrails and lamp posts were graceful and pleasing, largely thanks to Jesse Hartley, a rugged individualist appointed Dock Engineer in 1824. As bridgemaster for Yorkshire's West Riding, he had already displayed a determination for the best in design and workmanship. Bridge contractors feared his appearance on a site, where his sharp eyes weighed every detail against his own meticulous standards.

He ruled over the growth of Liverpool dockland like a dictator, "rough in manner and occasionally even rude, using expletives which even the angel of mercy would not like to record; sometimes capricious and tyrannical, but occasionally where he was attacked, a firm and unswerving friend". Albert Dock was his greatest achievement, built at a cost of £722,000 and opened by a genial Prince Albert in July 1845. Built round a rectangular dock, this enclosed system of five-storey fireproof warehouses, their ground floors flanked by a colonnade of squat and massive cast iron columns, enabled goods to be transferred directly from ship to storeroom, eliminating damage and pilferage during the operation.

A spectacular increase in the city's trade and fortunes followed the creation of the docks, together with an army of people in search of work. Their numbers were swelled by immigration from Ireland; 300,000 refugees from that famine-stricken island landed at Liverpool in 1847 alone. The demand for cheap accommodation was overwhelming and five thousand destitutes crammed the city's workhouse. Fortunes for the few were quickly made by throwing up row upon row of cheap back-to-back terraces, with no through ventilation.

Kitty Wilkinson spent much of her life helping the poor of Liverpool and fighting the pitifully inadequate conditions in which they lived. An

The Anglican Cathedral, Liverpool, designed by Sir Giles Gilbert Scott

unofficial district nurse, social worker and welfare officer rolled into one, she was called out to help at all hours of the day and night and, because of her own working-class background, welcomed as a friend. Her night school, where she taught destitute children to read, was financed by daytime work, washing, sewing and, on more than one occasion, the sale of horse droppings gathered from the city streets.

When cholera swept through the poor parts of Liverpool in 1832 and 1833, Kitty Wilkinson prevented the disease from reaching disaster level by applying elementary principles of fresh air and cleanliness. She turned her tiny kitchen into a wash house for poor neighbours, using soap and chloride of lime as a simple disinfectant. Later she transferred the operation to a large cellar, and in one week the wash load included "34 beds, 140 dozen of clothes, 158 shirts, 110 blankets and 60 quilts". She may rightly be considered the inventor of public wash houses and their launderette successors.

Time lends romance to the backbreaking drudgery of this kind of charitable work. An artist's impression of Kitty Wilkinson, printed in an old memoir, shows a pretty young woman, fair face unlined and hands soft and supple. The photograph used as the model for her memorial window in Liverpool Cathedral shows the real Kitty, black browed,

Anglican Gothic facing Roman Catholic contemporary, Liverpool

the face drawn and wrinkled. Her hands, once gracefully tiny, are swollen and calloused, the fingers spread in pain.

Pubs were the most splendid and comfortable buildings known to the poor of Victorian Liverpool, ornate and flamboyant places clad in brightly decorated tiles with lights warmly glowing through coloured glass. Most were built after the 1830 Beer House Act, a valiant attempt to deflect drinking habits from spirits to beer. In Liverpool the attempt failed, for the city magistrates retained the right to grant spirit and beer licences and encouraged landlords to apply for both. Once the Act became law, licences were issued at the brisk rate of fifty a day, and the consumption of both spirits and beer rose alarmingly.

Too late, the magistrates tried to alter course. They would, they said, grant a beer-only licence to anyone of good character. The result was a foregone conclusion. Beer sales soared even higher, with no corresponding decline in the consumption of spirits. In 1866 a hundred Liverpool children were suffocated by drunken parents. Twenty years later the National Temperance League reported: "Liverpool is pre-eminent for drunkenness and crime in proportion to its population over every other seaport in the country".

Like Manchester, Liverpool is a city in decline. It seems to have lost the thrust, vitality and dogged determination that transformed an insignificant coastal town into one of the world's largest ports and commercial centres. In the arts, however, it still reflects its traditional genius. The famous painter George Stubbs was followed a century later by Augustus John, whose controversial portraits were too advanced for the city council at the time. Sir Adrian Boult and Sir Malcolm Sargent were both distinguished conductors of the Liverpool Philharmonic Orchestra, and Alan Rawsthorne, one of Britain's leading contemporary composers, grew up in the city. Nathaniel Hawthorne, author and one-time United States consul in Liverpool is followed, in a different style, by Nicholas Monserrat, son of a Rodney Street doctor.

Of all Liverpool's sons who have made their mark in the world, perhaps the most eccentric was Joseph Williamson. On his death in 1840 he left behind a bewildering network of tunnels thrusting deep into the sandstone below his Edge Hill home. His passages which lead nowhere were punctuated by hand-hewn caverns, follies of a life-time's fruitless endeavour.

Sand, the scourge of the Mersey, is what makes the nearby coast so attractive and invests it with an outsize problem. The ten miles of dunes beyond Crosby were relatively inaccessible not so long ago, when only a few roads struck out to the sea. At Ainsdale, the dunes were a nature-lover's paradise, carpeted with rare flowers and the haunt of birds, red squirrels, lizards and the largest colony of natterjack toads in the country. Small boys collected them by the sackful to sell in Lancashire pet shops.

Marram grass, protected by law on the Lancashire coast since 1740, stabilised the dunes, although stiff winds from the sea shifted the sand about at an alarming rate. On a day of fierce spring gales in 1912, one dune increased its height by fourteen feet and its length by over fifty feet. Marram's restraining influence on the dunes depends on its ability to draw moisture from the sand, and along this coast it is drying out. Lack of water, urban development and uncontrolled tramping out by sightseers have freed the sand from its stabilising grasses. Blowing freely, it destroys trees and plants in its path, threatens older dunes, chokes streams and smothers fields. Southport, or at least many of its visitors, are partly to blame for the devastation of the dunes, and the conflict between the preservation of natural life and the needs of a holiday town is hard to reconcile.

Sand, paradoxically the Lancashire coast's biggest attraction and its most wearisome burden, set Southport on the way to prosperity. Just as quickly, it threatened to take away the town's livelihood. In Lord Street

71

a stone marks the site of Duke's Folly, opened in 1792 by Old Duke, more properly called William Sutton. Duke's Folly was Southport's first inn, and when Old Duke ferried his customers down to the sea in horse-drawn carts, only a few yards separated the shore from deep water.

Prosperity came slowly to the town, and it required the appearance of royalty to make the place fashionable for respectable people of substance. From the start, the resort was developed to attract select and preferably well-to-do residents and visitors.

Southport's seafront was lined with solid residences, each with its own extensive and well-tended garden. Lord Street became the North's most fashionable street; dignity and respectability were unshaken characteristics of the town by the middle of the nineteenth century. Then nature took a hand. The sea started to withdraw, leaving an ever increasing width of mud between the promenade and the water. A long pier was built to reach the tide line, so long that one had to be fit, and preferably young, to walk its length. A miniature train was provided for the less agile.

About 1880, in a further attempt to retrieve the situation, the mud flats were hidden under a marine lake, but it was too late. By then Blackpool's miles of spendid sand, freshly washed twice a day by a constant sea, had enticed visitors away and Southport never regained its glory.

Although Southport now has its pleasure beach, its ice cream stands and hotdog carts, and even 'kiss-me-quick'-hatted trippers, they look out of place among Victorian villas and Edwardian hotels. The town's undeniable charm has much to do with its faded gentility and nostalgic echoes of a stiffly respectable past.

Between Southport's sea and the first Lancashire fells, lies a curious countryside, a spread of open fields where sunlight glitters on greenhouse glass, until industry is encountered at Wigan and Hindley. Buffeted by coastal winds and owing allegiance more to the sea than to the inland landscape, it would be reasonable to assume that it was flat, like the neighbouring Fylde, but it is not. One writer accurately described this part of Lancashire as the "country of little hills", sudden and unexpected eruptions like Parbold, only a few hundred feet high, from whose summit you can gaze not only across the level plain to the sea, but also away to the distant Welsh hills and the dark fells of Yorkshire.

This part of Lancashire is watered by the Douglas and the Yarrow, two rivers that join forces near Croston and flow in unison into the Ribble mouth. The Douglas was one of the first rivers to attract the attention of the canal builders. Spurred by the prospect of cheap transport to the Ribble, Wigan coal owners tackled the river early in the eighteenth

Liverpool Playhouse, the old theatre next to the new restaurant

century, widening its banks and excavating cuts to make it a speedy and easily navigable waterway. It soon proved inadequate for the flow of traffic, and a canal, part of the Leeds and Liverpool waterway, was constructed parallel to the river.

Wigan's coal mines, Lancashire's priming pump as the Industrial Revolution gathered momentum, were once little more than curiosities for distinguished visitors. As late as the eighteenth century, city ladies and their gentlemen were expressing surprise that coal would burn brightly, and were more interested in intricate salt cellars, ink stands and boxes fashioned from this unusual fossil, polished to a jet-like brilliance that amazingly left no trace of dirt on the fingers.

If hearing its name raises a smile up and down the country, Wigan can afford to shrug indifferently. Industry may have robbed it of its early beauty, but it can look back with satisfaction to a long and honourable history. Nearly 1,500 years ago a valiant Celt, King Arthur himself according to local people, fought a savage battle against invaders who had strayed far from their Yorkshire settlements to the banks of the Douglas.

The Romans knew the area well, and as a Royalist stronghold,

73

St John's beacon, the tower landmark of Liverpool's new shopping centre

Wigan was in the thick of the Civil War strife. Lord Derby returned from the Isle of Man in 1651 to captain the Royalist forces in their last great northern battle against the Roundheads. King Charles' forces were soundly defeated, and the noble lord managed to escape with a small band of men. He rejoined the young King at Worcester, again tasting defeat before heading back to the comparative safety of the north. He was unlucky, and his captors brought him to Chester, where he was found guilty of treason and sentenced to death in the place where he was most hated. His scaffold was built in Bolton's market square, the town he had pillaged and whose citizens he had slaughtered less than ten years earlier.

Mab's Cross and the Bradshaw tomb in Wigan's parish church are links in an odd story. In 1314, Sir William Bradshaw left Haigh Hall and his wife, Mabel, to fight in a Scots uprising. His return was expected within weeks, but the rebellion was a troublesome one, and took three years to crush. Still Sir William did not return home, and his wife assumed he had been killed in battle or executed. She waited another seven years before remarrying, this time to Sir Osmund Nevill, a Welsh knight. However, her first husband was still alive, though outlawed. After his pardon, he returned to Haigh to find his wife married to another. He decided to see how she had settled into her new life and, disguised as a palmer from the Holy Land, went along to Haigh Hall. Mabel, no doubt rivetted with surprise, recognised him and told her new husband, who beat her soundly and called her a fool. Sir William promptly revealed his identity, challenged the ursurper to combat and killed him outside the Hall. As a penance for her supposed sin of bigamy, Mabel Bradshaw's confessor made her make a weekly pilgrimage to Wigan Cross, midway between the town and Haigh, walking barefoot, wound in a penance sheet and carrying a lighted candle, thus explaining the origin of Mab's Cross.

Still along the course of the Douglas, Mawdesley can be hard to find unless you know the way. It plays hide-and-seek in a network of country lanes at the foot of Harrock Hill, which perhaps explains why the modern world seems to have passed it by. History and legend play a large part in the Mawdesley story, and if you like ghostly tales talk to an old Mawdesleyan - he'll tell you plenty.

The Black Bull inn is a good place to start. Only its Tudor windows speak of its antiquity and, sadly, its famous open fireplace, an immense thing called Hell Hob, has long since gone. Some villagers still claim to have sat round the hob of hell, but today the only reminder is a giant poker, weighing 16 lbs and long enough to prod the fires of Hades without burning your fingers.

Haigh Hall, Wigan

Almost next door is Mawdesley Hall, reached by a short flight of worn steps half hidden in the grass verge. In a carved balcony at the top of the steps a small peephole still looks out on to the road below, allowing a wary eye to be kept on travellers. During the troubled days of the Civil War, a cannon's snout poked out of the peephole, permanently trained on the highway.

The Hall is still occupied, but its oldest part, the Tudor central hall, is sadly decayed. The beautiful plasterwork and wood panelling, the armorial bearings of the Mawdesley family over the huge fireplace, the original heavy timber front door with its huge wrought-iron lock and key, all remain, but are gradually falling into extreme disrepair. The occupant recently suggested that plans were afoot to put the place to rights, as befits a priceless and beautiful piece of Lancashire history.

Less than three miles away, Rufford is still a quiet backwater, although traffic on the Liverpool to Preston trunk road thunders past within earshot. In 1836, Baines wrote of Rufford: "The habits of the people are simple and unsophisticated, and their manners much more bland and agreeable than in the manufacturing villages. The superintending eye of a paternal landlord is visible, and there are here all the indications of ancient family dignity sustained and heightened by modern improvements".

The Black Bull Inn, Mawdesley

Paternal landlordism came to an end a century later, when Lord Hesketh transferred Rufford Old Hall to the National Trust, but Rufford folk are still gentle and agreeable and seem less concerned than most about material things.

The Old Hall of the Heskeths is sandwiched between the main road and the canal, the original fifteenth-century timber hall linked to a brick wing of 1662 by nineteenth-century offices. It is impressive from the outside, with the timber frame supported by a massive beam resting on a low stone plinth. The black and white pattern with quatrefoil decorations is broken by mullioned and latticed windows and a splended octagonal bay window with coved eaves.

Inside, the 46 feet long Great Hall has hardly changed since it was built over five hundred years ago. It must be the noblest medieval interior in Lancashire, and has managed to retain its original movable screen, a gigantic Tudor draught excluder once a common feature of great magpie houses in Lancashire and Cheshire. Seven feet wide and almost as tall, the height doubled by three extravagantly carved finials, this monster of a screen kept the most searching blasts from reaching the Hesketh family and their guests seated at the high table, but it must have required an army of men to move it when the wind changed direction.

Rufford also brings to mind Speke Hall, another fifteenth-century black and white hall, now sited uncomfortably close to Liverpool airport. Larger and grander than Rufford Old Hall, Speke is fortunate to be looking still across the Mersey. With the extinction of the male line in 1731, this old home of the Norris family passed to Mary, who married Lord Sidney Beauclerk. Known to his friends as 'Worthless Sidney', he spent his money and more, neglected his new home and drove his wife to suicide in the dark depths of the moat. In turn, Beauclerk's son and grandson left Speke to rot, and by 1797, less than seventy years after it had passed from Norris hands, it was fast becoming a ruin.

In the year when Richard Watt bought Speke, a relative described its condition at the time: "The house was very much damaged by the people the Beauclerks allowed to live there. The large carved panels, in common with the rest of the wainscote in the Great Hall, were much broken and defaced, one half of them being split down the middle and taken out. All the tapestry, and an inlaid oak floor belonging to the Great Parlour having been taken to pieces, the former for horse blankets, the latter for firewood."

No wonder that much of Richard Watt's fortune, made in the West Indies, was consumed in repairing the damage caused by years of Beauclerk ownership. But whatever their feelings towards the Beauclerks, the

Mawdesley Hall

Watts family never lost sight of the long Norris connection with Speke. On her death in 1921, Adelaide Watt left Speke in trust for members of the Watt family for 21 years, and in 1942 the property passed to the National Trust.

On its way to join the Douglas, the Yarrow wanders past Chorley, less of a key-link in north-south communications since the building of the motorways. By the early nineteenth century, the growth of turnpike roads had made Chorley a vital staging post between north and south, and every day a complement of coaches from Manchester and London, bound for Carlisle or even deep into Scotland, pulled into the inn yards of this prosperous market town.

Nearby, Astley Hall, where Elizabethan half timbering has been replaced by Jacobean brick and stone, seems all twinkling glass, every flash and wink from diamond panes faithfully duplicated by the lake. Cromwell's bed is here, a stately four-poster that rested the Lord Protector of the Commonwealth after the battle of Preston in August, 1648. An unusual treasure is in the Long Hall, a shovel board nearly 24 feet long. Here family and friends gathered to throw, or 'shovel', metal weights into marked spaces on the board, but sadly the rules of the game seem to have been lost with the passage of time.

Closer to our own day was Henry Tate, born in Chorley in 1819, a

Astley Hall, Chorley

The Long Hall at Astley Hall, Chorley

grocer's assistant until he moved to Liverpool and sugar refining. In middle age he acquired a method of cutting loaf sugar into tiny cubes, and quickly went on to dominate the sugar market and make the fortune that later built and endowed London's Tate Gallery.

Eccleston stands close to the Yarrow, the church that gives the village its name being the successor to others stretching back to Anglian times. Not much more than a mile away by river, but twice as far by road, Croston's fifteenth-century church also overlooks the Yarrow. The tower is splendidly framed between old cottages on either side of a cobbled lane, and a stone bridge curves across the river whose flood water, according to a churchwardens' report of 1710, was responsible for undermining the massive church pillars.

Whether or not Croston takes its name from Cross Toan - and the broken base of the market cross, raised on three steps, can still be seen - it is certainly one of Lancashire's oldest towns, its history going back to well before the Norman Conquest. It was identified on a primitive map

Fifteenth-century Church at Croston

Carr House, Bretherton; Jeremiah Horrocks was the first man to see
and record the transit of Venus in front of the sun in 1639
— from the room above the porch

of 1094 as a village with a market cross, and it is impossible to wander
along its largely unspoilt streets without seeing evidence of the past,
often tidily dated; Henry and Isobel Croston's almshouses (1692); the
packhorse bridge (1682); the rebuilt grammar school (1660).

Yarrow and Douglas soon meet at Bretherton. Nearby Carr House
was less than thirty years old when Jeremiah Horrocks lodged there, the
new curate at Much Hoole church and destined to be better known as
the Father of British Astronomy. From his blacked-out room above
Carr House porch, Horrocks squinted through his primitive telescope
and saw a black spot pass in front of the sun, the first sighting of the
transit of Venus. The date and time are recorded: 3.15 on the afternoon
of Sunday, 24th November 1639. Horrocks died two years later, aged
twenty-three.

When the demolition men were about to move into Carr House in the
1950s, Barry Elder and his wife, Jean, were running a dolls' hospital in
London. One of their customers, as a token of gratitude, insisted on giving them a priceless German china doll. Fascinated by its expressive fea-
tures and delicate workmanship, the Elders went on to build the biggest

collection of dolls in the country. Housing them was a problem and, quite by chance, Lady Lilford read about the collection and linked it with Carr House. With great determination she persuaded the Ministry of Works and other public bodies to restore the old house and in April 1966, it opened as the Barry Elder doll museum.

Mrs Elder looks after about 1,200 dolls, the biggest four feet tall and the smallest a half-inch figure originally sold in a tiny wooden egg as an Easter doll. Many are shown in a series of tableaux using period furniture and settings and, of course, Mrs Elder is always on the look-out for new dolls.

Beyond Bretherton, the river runs past Tarleton towards the Ribble and along the edge of Martin Mere, an odd name for what appears, and indeed is, rich agricultural land. But until the end of the eighteenth century, it was a shallow lake, eighteen miles in circumference and a source of real peril to those who ventured along the vague tracks criss-crossing the water.

In 1693, Thomas Fleetwood of Bank Hall began draining the lake, an ambitious scheme that proved beyond the technical competence and pockets of Fleetwood and his neighbouring landowners. A century later Thomas Eccleston of Scarisbrick tried again, this time successfully. Trenches and sluices overcame the problem of the Ribble's tidal waters, and floodgates with an ingenious paddle device kept the system free from mud and sand. By 1784 corn and grass were growing where water stood a few years earlier, and within his lifetime Thomas Eccleston saw his prime cattle grazing rich grassland that once had been sour, waterlogged waste.

6 · BLACKPOOL TO LYTHAM AND FLEETWOOD

"Safe and sure trips to Hell" was how the Lancashire clergy described the first Sunday rail excursions to Blackpool. That was in 1840, when passengers on the newly opened Preston and Wyre Railway could leave the train at Poulton and take a horse carriage into Blackpool.

Fifty years earlier Blackpool hardly merited a mention on the map. The biggest type was kept for Bispham, a mile or two north of the stream that drained Marton Moss into the sea and whose chocolate coloured water gave a name to a cluster of cottages. These were little more than crude clay shelters, each with a beaten earth floor, a hearth in the centre of the only room and a hole in the roof to let the smoke out.

After the Romans left Lancashire, Bispham became an Anglian settlement, *Biscopham*, the home of the Celtic bishop. It was included in the Domesday Survey and before long monasteries at Shrewsbury and Leek owned much of its lands. Later the manor was held by the Butler family, until the reign of Henry VIII, when it was sold to the Fleetwoods and then to the Cliftons of Lytham. As late as the nineteenth century, Bispham was still an attractive village, its white-painted houses shadowed by overhanging thatch. Many of these three-bay dwellings were built round stout timber crucks, prefabricated arches introduced to the Fylde by the Norse invaders a thousand years ago.

The Butler family's title to the manor of Bispham included Layton, Norbreck and *le pull*, the pool, the first recorded mention of the place destined to become Britain's biggest holiday resort. By 1700 Blackpool was a huddle of cobble huts built on high clay cliffs overlooking the Irish Sea. Parish registers show the gradual development of family names, as daughters were sent inland to find a marriage partner. But Blackpool was still at the back of beyond, lacking proper communications with the prosperous inland towns and living a very primitive life under extremely arduous conditions.

Isolation made Blackpool and the Fylde a refuge for families like the

Blackpool's famous tower, golden sands and inevitable donkeys

Tyldesleys of Fox Hall, the Cliftons of Lytham and the Rigbys of Layton. All were Catholic families who clung to their religion, sheltering priests and maintaining their own private chapels.

A few brave souls ventured to Blackpool in the eighteenth century to sample its invigorating air. They were glad to buy overnight accommodation at one of the cottages, often sharing a bed with as many as twelve others. Provisions had to be fetched from Bispham or from inland farms. There were no shops at Blackpool, neither were there "donkey, pony, gig, car, or any other kind of conveyance". The only entertainment was a stroll along a grass promenade 600 feet long and 20 feet wide between the shore and the cottages.

Slowly the place prospered. It soon had its stage terminus, bathing house, post office and lending library. The lodging houses advertised their comforts in the Manchester papers and in 1795 the *Blackburn Mail* described Blackpool as "the first watering place in the kingdom", anticipating its future role as a centre of entertainment by announcing that "a Company of Comedians is shortly expected". Even so, it was not to everyone's taste. A spinster lady of thirty-two had this to say about her first visit: "Blackpool is situated on a level dreary moorish coast; the cliffs are of earth and not very high. It consists of a few houses ranged in line with the sea and four of these are for the reception of company. One accommodates thirty, one sixty and one eighty and the other a hundred persons. We were strangers all, and on the recommendation of the master of the Inn at Preston we drove to the house of eighty which is called Lane's End. The company now consisted of about seventy and I never found myself in such a mob. The people sat down to table behind their knives and forks to be ready for their dinner, while my mother, my father and myself, who did not choose to scramble, stood behind until someone more considerate than the rest made room for us. These people are, in general, of a species called Boltoners, whose coarseness of manners is proverbial even among their countrymen. The other houses are frequented by better company, that is Lancashire gentry, Liverpool merchants and Manchester manufacturers. I find here that I have no equals but the lawyers, for those who are my equals in fortune are distinguished by their vulgarity, and those who are my equals in manners are above me in situation."

At the height of the 1830 season, Blackpool attracted about a thousand visitors and the grass promenade had been worn down to a gravel strip. By 1850 its resident population of two thousand doubled during the season. The 1851 the Lancashire Directory sang its praises: "None here need complain of lassitude or ennui - there is amusement and employment for all. The horseman, pedestrian, the geologist, the concholigist and zoologist may ever find occupation on the shore and the herbalist on the land. The laying out of streets and walks, the erection of handsome houses and shops on every side, the establishment of elegant hotels and billiards, news and coffee rooms ... bespeak the rising importance of the town". As a warning, perhaps, to well brought-up young spinsters conscious of their social standing, the Directory added darkly: "The months of September and October are considered the genteel season."

Twenty years later Blackpool's population had grown fourfold, bringing with it piped water, two piers and Uncle Tom's Cabin, with its swings, roundabouts and inevitable Victorian photographer. Among the town's many attractions at that time, pride of place must go to the Raikes Hall Pleasure Gardens. Concealed in its forty acres of terraces, walks and flower gardens, were a race track, boating and fishing lakes, a monkey house, dance halls and a fairground. No less than seventeen bars were provided to assuage the thirst created by such vigorous activ-

An attractive corner near Cottam, on the edge of the Fylde

ity. Blondin performed his high wire act here for a short season, carrying his adult son on his back across the rope. Raikes Hall Gardens lingered on until the end of the century, when they had already been surpassed by newer and more exciting novelties.

The replacement of the grass promenade with flagged esplanades along the sea front had been going on since 1860; the North Shore Promenade was opened in 1899 and the South Promenade six years later. The total cost was £440,000. Blackpool has never lacked ambition or the willingness to spend money. Engineering problems were immense. Extending the promenade a hundred feet into the sea meant digging deep into the sand to find bedrock, conquering quicksands and building a massive wall designed to withstand the worst the sea could hurl at it.

Among the new amusements, the Winter Gardens was famous for its knockabout variety shows. But it also nodded at culture by staging concerts of serious music; Melba, Tettrazini and Caruso were no strangers to Blackpool. In 1909 Caruso was able to fix a fee of £1,000 for a single performance. As Manager, Bill Holland decided to carpet the Winter Gardens for £100. His friends tried to dissuade him. Carpets for the trippers? He was assured they would only spit on them. In true Blackpool fashion he turned the taunt to his own advantage: "Come to the Winter

Gardens and spit on Bill Holland's carpets", he advertised. The trippers came in droves and, overawed by the rich grandeur of their surroundings, kept to their best behaviour.

Prompted by the popularity of M. Eiffel's strange tower in Paris, the Blackpool Tower Company was formed in 1891. Three years later Blackpool Tower was open for business; the problem of what to do when it rained was solved. Tucked snugly between its four immense legs, the Tower Circus accommodated three thousand people at each performance. Thousands more thronged its pavilion and the higher platforms. Almost as impressive was the Big Wheel, opened in 1896 next to the Winter Gardens. It rose over 200 feet into the air, weighed about 1,000 tons and its heavy axle rested on columns embedded in 9 feet of concrete. Each of its thirty carriages carried as many passengers and at the top of its circle you could see far out over the ocean and across the whole of the Fylde flatlands.

It would be pleasant to record that Blackpool has never looked back from these adventurous Victorian days, when the Lancashire working man spent his annual holiday with his family amidst the resort's breathtaking amusements. Then its appeal was to the young and boisterous; today its attraction lies largely among the middle-aged and the elderly. Recently Blackpool lost enough confidence in itself to commission a market-survey of visitors. Although it attracted nearly six million in 1972 (who between them spent £70 million) only one in ten were visiting the town for the first time, and almost half had holidayed there ten times or more. Perhaps the sun is at last setting on the world's most famous Golden Mile, or more likely, there will be a shift of emphasis in the town. Blackpool's long term future may lie more with industry than holidaymakers, or possibly an uneasy alliance of the two.

Trial drills have raised hopes of large fields of natural gas, and perhaps oil, off the Lancashire coast. British Gas is drilling 25 miles from Blackpool Tower, and major oil companies have concessions to drill over an area stretching from North Wales to beyond Morecambe. Blackpool watches the drilling operations with mixed feelings, anxiety on the one hand that oil spillage and the paraphernalia of a new industry could kill the resort as a holiday attraction, anticipation on the other that oil and gas finds on the scale of those in the North Sea could transform the town almost overnight into a major air- and seaport.

To see what Blackpool looked like in its pre-concrete days, go a little farther down the coast to Lytham. Here the grass promenade has been preserved, together with a quiet dignity more akin to Southport than to Blackpool. Both, in fact, were Lytham's rivals and in the end Blackpool won the battle with its strand of firm, golden sand. Natural silting of the

Ribble created Lytham's inglorious mud flats, and work on the river mouth to build Preston docks in the nineteenth century only accelerated the process.

Lytham's Regency and Victorian elegance contrasts strongly with the Edwardian houses of its near neighbour, St Anne's, a town largely created in the early years of the present century. St Anne's owes its existence to successful Lancashire merchants who, having made their 'brass' in the smoky streets of industrial towns, decided to forsake the muck and take their money to a pleasanter spot. Once a regular train service guaranteed that they could travel to Manchester daily and in comfort, they came in their hundreds, building large and solid mansions behind the sand dunes.

Inland from the holiday coast lies the Fylde, bounded on the north by the Lune and to the south by the Ribble. As if water on three sides is not enough, it is split from west to east along the middle by the Wyre, its broad mouth guarded by Fleetwood and Knott End. A Roman port once stood here, Portus Setantiorum, long nibbled to nothing by coastal erosion, but a splendid starting point if the legions ever intended to invade Ireland.

Vanished Rome has long been replaced by modern Fleetwood. Looking out from the spacious rooms of Rossall Hall, Sir Peter Hesketh-Fleetwood saw a wilderness of marsh, sandhills and rough grass, and he dreamed of a splendid new town built here at the mouth of the Wyre, a

Glasson dock, once a major Lancashire port and now
largely used as a boating marina

port bigger than either Preston or Lancaster. He had been present in 1830 when the Duke of Wellington opened the Manchester to Liverpool railway and had been impressed, like many others, with the new form of travel.

Five years later, his architect Decimus Burton had built a Chinese pavilion on a small hill overlooking the sea and was marking out the line of the new town's main streets with a horse-drawn plough. Funds had been raised for extending the railway to the new town, and by 1842 infant Fleetwood had a population of almost 3,000. By that time, unfortunately, Sir Peter had run out of cash and outside developers took over. Rossall Hall became a public school, but despite setbacks the new town and port began to prosper. A fishing industry was established and still remains a vital part of the town's activities. Fleetwood's fishing is still in the big league. Small boats fish home waters for plaice, herring, mackerel and prawns, as they have since the town began. So, too, have the near-water trawlers, middling-sized vessels returning to port regularly with fresh fish. Most recent are the freezer ships that venture into the deepest seas, staying longer from their home port and quick-freezing their catches as soon as they hit the deck.

For a time, Fleetwood also marked the end of the London to Glasgow railway line; from here the *Fire King* took passengers by sea to Scotland. Monday, 20th September 1847, set the seal of approval on the new town. To a salute of twenty-one guns, the Royal Yacht made its way uncertainly into the mouth of the Wyre and anchored at Fleetwood. Queen Victoria and Prince Albert, accompanied by the Prince of Wales and the Princess Royal, held court in a huge temporary reception hall on the quay, red carpeted and draped in crimson. Although the occasion was invested with State ceremonial and pageantry, Victoria had a more practical reason for her visit. The new trains provided her with a much quicker way of travelling from Balmoral to Buckingham Palace, and the trip south from Fleetwood marked the start of royal enthusiasm for rail travel.

Tides along the Lancashire coast can be something of a menace, rising and falling as much as thirty feet or more. Sir Peter Hesketh-Fleetwood's marshes had been flooded early in the nineteenth century, but little attention was paid to this hazard when his new town was being built. A high tide backed by a hurricane wind damaged much of Fleetwood in 1852, and in the next hundred years the place was flooded five times. A line chiselled on a hotel doorway marks the height of the most serious flood in 1927, when winds transformed an expected 27 feet tide into a monstrous 34 feet tearaway that swamped 2,000 acres and marooned the town for four days.

Green Park, Blackburn, freshly landscaped to feature the canal

Despite its youth, Fleetwood can claim one distinguished son. Rossall Hall, from which Sir Peter looked out on the site of his new town, was also the birthplace of William Allen in 1532. At the age of fifteen he went to Oxford and became a Fellow three years later. In Queen Mary's reign he was appointed Principal of St Mary's Hall and a Canon of York, but retired hurriedly to Louvain when Elizabeth came to the throne.

He came back to Lancashire briefly in 1565, a risky business, and stayed with the Heskeths at Mains Hall in the heart of the Fylde. On his return to the Continent he was made Archbishop of Mechlin and Cardinal patron of a Naples abbey. He was also named Protector of English Catholics, and helped to change the old English Hospice for pilgrims in Rome into a college for church students from his native land. It remains such today, and its old students still fill the key positions in the Roman Catholic Hierarchy of England and Wales.

When the Mains Hall kitchens were knocked down a number of priests' hiding holes were discovered, in one of which "were manifest tokens of its having been occupied". The vicar of Blackpool visited the house in 1835, and in an oratory off the drawing room found fragments of illuminated missals and relics of saints, together with a stick (perhaps a crozier?) carved with a Cardinal's cap and the date 1626. Mains Hall is also remembered as the home of Mrs Fitzherbert, who came here in retirement after her marriage to King George IV was put aside.

Within living memory fishermen hooked pearl mussels from the bed of the Wyre at Knott End but there is no point in trying to make a fortune at it now, although you will still find plenty of ordinary shellfish. Old charts called the Wyre a safe anchorage, a welcome haven for small boats plying between long-forgotten ports before the days of decent roads, canals and railways.

In their rush to reach the sea, few people recognise the beauty of the Wyre landscape. A couple of centuries ago it was rough land, divided from the sea by unattractive bogs and marshes. Small hamlets were linked by unsurfaced tracks and their sparse populations lived as best they could from modest crops of barley, beans and oats. They knew little of the world beyond the Fylde and cared even less.

The draining of the Ribble mosslands changed the character of the landscape, if not the people. New roads ride high above the so-called bottomless marshes, which now support rich cereal crops. Acres of glasshouses make the Fylde the market garden of Lancashire and beyond, growing tomatoes, cucumbers and lettuces for much of England. Close to the coast, nothing escapes the bracing sea winds; like the people, trees and hedges lean permanently towards the fells. Further inland, where the countryside is more sheltered, the villages are old and the winding lanes even older.

A few yards from an arched stone bridge over the Wyre, the village of St Michael's is named after the fifteenth-century church; the church preceded the village, like its neighbour at nearby Churchtown. Paulinus, Bishop of York, is said to have founded St Michael's church in the seventh century, and twelve hundred years later official records either ignored the village or it did not exist.

Garstang is not far away, where the Fylde ends as it meets the motorway. Its old-fashioned streets betray an antiquity that goes back beyond a Roman presence. Oddly, the older houses are numbered both outside and inside the front doors, and the two numbers do not tally. The one outside is the usual number required by the Authority for the use of postmen. The inside number was fixed so that the owner's agent could collect his rents, although how he managed to identify a house when the door was firmly closed is another matter.

Halfway between Preston and Lancaster, and just about midway between Manchester and Kendal, Garstang was a major stopping point on the northern coach road. In the 1820s, from Manchester's Market Street to the Royal Oak at Garstang took six hours. Between them, the

Royal Oak and its neighbour, the Eagle and Child, coped with twelve coaches a day. While the horses were being changed and the mailbags loaded, passengers shared a welcome meal and a glass before summoning strength for another six-hour haul to Kendal.

Although Garstang once flirted with industry, trying its hand at hats and cotton goods, its trade has always rested on animals and agriculture. It raised Wyresdale cattle - small, with curled hair and wide horns - and its powerful Shire horses provided much of Lancashire's motive power before the arrival of the internal combustion engine.

On its way from Garstang from the fells, the Wyre passes the ruined site of Greenhalgh Castle, the reward of the first Earl of Derby for stealing the dead King Richard's crown at Bosworth Field and placing it on the head of the victorious Bolingbroke. A licence from Henry VII authorised him to fortify "his manor of Greenhall in the parish of Garstang" for all time, without impediment or obstruction. But this "pretty castle of the Lords of Derbys", as Leland described it, survived for little more than a hundred years. It was already a ruin in 1643 when it was hurriedly refurbished and garrisoned to support King Charles in his battle against the Parliamentary forces. One of the last two Lancashire strongpoints to hold out, it finally surrendered after the death of its last Governor and the place was dismantled stone by stone.

Between Garstang and Blackpool a side road turns off through Poulton-le-Fylde, once the Wyre's principal port. Ships anchored here from as far away as Russia, and as befitted a place of substance and importance it had its own Customs House and Quarter Session. Beyond Poulton the road crosses the Wyre at Shard Bridge, where earlier a ferry had replaced a Roman ford. A nearby notice lists the original tolls laid down by the Shard Bridge Act of 1862; a penny for foot passengers, and threepence for a private carriage. If you were herding a score of cattle at the time, the toll-keeper extracted a further one shilling and sixpence. Crossing the Wyre in those days was quite an expensive proposition.

The road wanders northwards round the coast, through pretty Hambleton and across Pilling Moss to Cockerham and Glasson. This coastline, where the Irish Sea rushes in and out close to the Lune mouth, can be a treacherous place. Countless men have gone out on the marshes for a day's shooting and have failed to return. Darkness, a miscalculation about the tide and a lost sense of direction are fatal, either singly or in combination. Even the narrow motor road along the edge of the Moss is not as innocent as it looks. The warning signs about high tides should be observed, unless you want to ruin your car in a few feet of water.

For home use, farmers still cut out peaty turf as cheap winter fuel. Pilling's other sort of turf makes superb bowling greens. Countless scars near the road show where the grass, carefully sown and left for a few years to be washed by the tide and grazed by sheep, has been cut and taken inland to fetch a high price.

The coast also had its smugglers. Certainly the people of Pilling and Cockerham were keen wreck hunters, even down to the vicar who brought his service to an abrupt end when a wreck was announced. Willing hands stripped the stricken vessel, and most of the older coastal houses had their secret corners in which to conceal spirits, silks and tobacco from the prying eyes of the Customs men.

Cockerham still has its Vicar's Tide, when at certain times of the year the incumbent - in default of the ancient abbey at Cockersands - claims the right to trap salmon at the ebb of the morning tide. Only the Abbey's Chapter House still stands, turned into a family burial vault when the Daltons took over the monastery lands after Henry VIII ordered the monks to leave in 1539. In its day, Cockersands Priory was among the three greatest Abbeys in Lancashire. Because of its isolation, this spot was chosen as the site for a religious hospital. In the twelfth century, the Norbertines started to build a monastery, but it must have been a thankless job. As fast as they built, the sea washed the structure away and continuous repairs and strengthenings were the order of the day.

Things had improved by the fifteenth century. The Priory was an important place and it had its own quay, with beacons in the channel to guide in boats carrying visitors from abroad. Those visiting the place from the Fylde had a more difficult passage. Paths across the dangerous mosses were few and unsignposted, and anyone incautious enough to set off without a guide stood to lose both his way and his life.

At the mouth of the Lune, Glasson is another lost cause. This was Lancaster's own port, built towards the end of the eighteenth century when the higher reaches of the Lune became choked with silt. Linked with the Preston to Lancaster canal in 1825, smaller ships sailed through one dock and down to Preston on the waterway. Larger vessels discharged cargo from all over the world in a second dock. Glasson lost its trade to Preston and Fleetwood, a victim of the Victorian struggle for more and more trade and ever-increasing profits.

Today it is a pleasant backwater, and although a few foreign ships berth to discharge cargo, Glasson is mainly a marine for yachtsmen and others who love messing about in boats, or try the less-adventurous novelty of navigating long barges through the canal locks.

7 · PRESTON TO BLACKBURN

When Dicky Turner stuttered out his pledge against the demon drink, he unwittingly gave a new word to the language. An early recruit to John Livesey's temperance movement, Dicky publicly promised to abandon his drunken ways and become a t-t-t-total abstainer. Preston was the cradle of teetotalism; it gave the world its first temperance newspaper and its first temperance hotel.

Built on a slight rise, Preston commands the navigable waters of the Ribble and the open acres of the flat coastal plain. Its geographical position guaranteed commercial and political importance. Skulls and other bones dug up when the docks were being built in the 1880s were evidence of a settlement here more than 3,000 years ago; people who dwelt in simple shelters by the river, who fished its waters from dugout canoes and who hunted red deer in the nearby woods.

Although the Romans chose to build their station higher up the river at Ribchester, they must have known Preston well. Cargo and passenger boats passed by regularly, probably heaving to so that their crews could buy fish, keep an eye on the natives or simply gather local information. The Anglians came later, together with the Church and the title of Priest Town.

Preston's importance as an ecclesiastical centre was not allowed to hinder the development of trade or the pursuit of wealth. Its merchant guild was formed before the Norman Conquest, and its position was strengthened by charters from William and his successors. The Merchant Guild lends itself to fancy and romance as the instrument of fair dealing, immaculate craftsmanship and absolute honesty.

No doubt these were the ideals on which it was founded, but human nature tends to make practice mock the ideal. The guild operated to give merchants mutual trading support, rights over lands and punishments, and a prospect of making good any trading losses. It safeguarded the merchants' superior social position against threat from

Blackburn old and new

below, like the humble hawker who peddled his goods from street to street and from town to town, and maintained high profit margins by fixing prices and preventing out-of-town merchants undercutting them at Preston market.

Together with the later craft guilds, the merchants' guild left Preston with a quaint inheritance. Every twenty years the town tips its hat to the past and stages Preston Guild. The first was held in 1328, and the last in 1972; in between, 28 work-free days of pageantry, parades and pleasures have been whittled down to a week devoted to rather self-conscious processions and half-hearted social events. Sound commercial sense now dictates that shops and offices stay firmly open for most of Guild Week. A long tradition seems to be reaching its end, but not without leaving its permanent mark on the language, where "Once every Preston Guild" is the equivalent of "once in a blue moon" elsewhere.

In a tiny house not far from the Stonygate cockpit where Dicky Turner stammered about teetotalism, Richard Arkwright and a companion set about perfecting a spinning machine. Late night bypassers, puzzled by lighted windows, shadowy movements and strange noises, soon spread tales of witchcraft and sorcery. In a way they were right, because Arkwright's machine led inevitably to a vastly different textile industry whose new machinery was little short of magical to those accustomed to old-fashioned ways and, in its disregard for common humanity, seemingly touched by the devil's hand.

Preston hand-workers were innately conservative, and their readiness to smash new machines drove Arkwright to Nottingham, where he opened his first mill. Soon afterwards Preston workers found themselves making muslins under the broad roof of John Horrock's Yellow Factory. Many preferred to remain their own masters, handloom weaving in their cottage loft, their wives spinning in the kitchen and the children carding. Why fret if textiles were going through a bad patch? A step or two from the weaver's cottage door was his own plot of land, big enough to feed his family. Fierce independence and self-respect are a vital part of the Lancashire character, but the self-employed weaver stood no chance against a torrent of cheap cloth from machines that required no sleep, little tending, and were unable to answer back.

Mills and factories proclaim Preston a commercial power in the land; its public buildings announce that it remains Lancashire's administrative and political centre. There are few reminders of an earlier and more romantic history, when Royalty smiled on the town and their favours often proved more of a curse than a blessing. Determined to teach the English King a lesson, Robert Bruce and a band of ragged Scots fired the town in 1307. Twenty-five years later Henry III exacted his revenge, ? Edward 3 marching to Preston, where he reorganised his army by pressing the townspeople into service, and on to Scotland to butcher 20,000 poor souls near Hallidown Hall.

During the Civil War, Preston stood fast for the King and found itself middleman between the two sides. Parliamentary forces stormed the town and took possession, but not for long. Accompanied by a strong force, Lord Derby marched from Lathom Hall and compelled the occupying garrison to surrender, but not before he had his sport killing six hundred Roundheads within the hour.

After Cromwell won a major battle on the Ribble plain in 1648, retreating Royalists were slaughtered wholesale in Preston streets. But Prestonians clung to their cause with a stubborn determination that bordered on stupidity and foolhardiness. Hearing the news that Charles I had been executed, they promptly gathered in the market square and solemnly proclaimed his son as Charles II, King of England.

The Stuart flag was raised in 1715, when the Pretender seized the town. Jacobite forces thought themselves safe behind stoutly barricaded gates, although troops led by General Willis and General Carpenter surrounded Preston. The battle was long and bloody, every house and every street fought over with savage intensity. When the rebel leaders surrendered, their army gathered in the market square to throw down their weapons. Then they were marched off, some for shipment to America, the most important to London for execution on Tower Hill.

Not long after the battle, Daniel Defoe visited Preston, finding it "a fine town and tolerably full of people . . . but not so much, they say, as was before the late bloody action with the northern rebels". In fact, the town was damaged so badly that much of it had to be rebuilt, including the pleasant streets and squares that now lie at the back of Fishergate.

Blackburn is less than ten miles from Preston, but far removed in character. Its closeness to bleak moorland slopes may account for its dour, withdrawn air. It is an inward-looking town, grimy and down-at-heel in close-up, but impressive when viewed from a distant height. Blackburn people think there's no better place, and even well-intended criticism offends them. Until the local people get to know them, strangers are regarded with barely concealed distrust and suspicion.

When opportunity rapped loudly at Blackburn's door, wilful indifference and pure cussedness usually sent it packing smartly away. An ingrained reluctance to recognise anything good from outside the town must be largely responsible for the unhappier chapters in its history. Although the place was mentioned in Domesday Book, it took a knock when the Normans ignored it and made Clitheroe their headquarters. Blackburn stayed an insignificant farming town until Tudor times, when textiles were introduced and woollen weaving became a Blackburn home-industry. Experimental cotton weaving followed and by the end of the eighteenth century the town's weavers had abandoned wool. The flying shuttle had speeded up weaving, but spinning remained a problem until James Hargreaves invented his jenny, a machine that matched the output of a score of hand spinners.

Hargreaves was a Blackburn man, and by rights his native town should have gained by his inventiveness. It could have become the centre of Britain's spinning trade for the asking, but local hand spinners took the short view and destroyed Hargreaves's jenny because they feared it would make them redundant. Its reception at Nottingham was a little more encouraging, enough to persuade one or two men to set up mills in Blackburn. Like Hargreaves first jenny, the new machines were quickly smashed to pieces by the hammers of Blackburn spinners. The millowners learned a quick lesson, moving south to friendlier towns and ending Blackburn's chance of spinning dominance.

The town remained an important weaving centre, its social development very similar to that of other newly-industrialised Lancashire towns. Families not long off the farm were transformed into millowners and merchants, living in splendid town houses along King Street and at the back of Dukes Brow. Their new country homes, built in leafy glades not far from the town centre, gradually became blackened oases of Victorian splendour as industry quickly spread and surrounded them with factories and strings of back-to-back houses.

By the nineteenth century, Blackburn should have known on which side its bread was buttered. Its livelihood depended on textile machinery and, on past experience, improved machines spelt increased prosperity. Yet when a new mill was fitted out with dandy looms, far more efficient and productive than earlier models, history repeated itself and resurrected traditional fears. Operatives of the older machines decided to do something to stop what they judged to be inevitable unemployment. In April 1826 over 10,000 people rioted, the soldiers unable to stop them sweeping through the town, breaking into mills and smashing their looms with sledge-hammers. The rioters had a rare old time until the troops reformed and were able to use their swords to disperse the mob.

Floodlit Cathedral, Blackburn

As the nineteenth century lengthened, Blackburn cautiously lifted its head and looked farther than it had in the past. The new parish church, built in the year of the dandy riots, was soon to become a cathedral nave. Before 1850 the railway connected the town with the world beyond, and in 1851 Queen Victoria gave it status in the form of a Mayor and Corporation.

But poor old Blackburn, where success seems rarely to endure! In 1974, when other Lancashire cotton towns were helping themselves to new territory and status as metropolitan districts of the Greater Manchester county, Blackburn found herself stripped of civic independence and, as part of the new Lancashire county, ruled from Preston.

Between Preston and Blackburn the main road runs between two rivers, the Ribble and the Darwen. The latter joins the Ribble west of Walton-le-Dale, where before the coming of industry the clear, fast-flowing waters were bridged at a key point on the north road. Cromwell's men crossed it before the battle on the plain in 1648, when the northerners abandoned their equipment and baggage and fled home as fast as their legs would carry them.

General Willis massed his troops at the bridge before re-taking Preston from the Jacobites, and his prisoners later tramped back across the Darwen on their way to die in London or, if they were lucky, to the American colonies. Walton memories are long, and the appearance of the Young Pretender on the same bridge thirty years later was marked by an almost total lack of enthusiasm, justified a few days later when his disconsolate troops trudged back across the bridge, this time towards the north.

On a bend in the old Blackburn road, about three miles from Walton Bridge, an arrow-like drive rises to the low, crenellated walls of Hoghton Tower. A visit to the Tower left memories of dark and sombre public rooms, but bright and cosy private quarters. In its immense banqueting hall King James I is said to have been so impressed with the quality of the beef that he knighted the joint on the spot. "Arise Sir Loin", is the phrase he supposedly used on that jocular occasion; the dictionary takes a more pedestrian view and makes sirloin a corruption of *sur longe*.

Certainly the de Hoghton family did King James proud in August 1617. For three days the royal party was feasted, feted and entertained on a lavish scale. Thirty substantial dishes formed the first course of Sunday dinner, followed by a second course narrower in choice but larger in quantity. This was typical of three main meals served daily during the King's visit.

Sir Richard de Hoghton must have smiled wryly as he contemplated

100

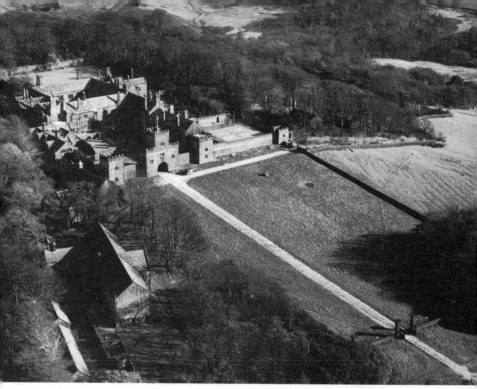

Hoghton Tower, where James I is supposed to have
knighted the beef as 'Sir Loin'

likely imprisonment for debt after the king's departure, for Hoghton
Tower was only second-best as far as James was concerned. He originally intended putting up at Barton Hall, north of Preston, but its
owner judged it cheaper to set fire to part of the house, and render it temporarily uninhabitable, rather than entertain His Majesty.

Cardinal Allen was a principal guest at the opening of the new Tower,
built to replace an old house down on the damp bank of the Darwen
river. The de Hoghtons paid dearly for this distinguished visitor a few
years later, when Queen Elizabeth enacted her laws against Catholics
and the practice of their religion. Under suspicion, Thomas de Hoghton
left the Tower and exiled himself in Flanders where he stayed, refusing a
royal pardon if he returned home and accepted the new religious situation. His half-brother, Richard, was imprisoned for sheltering the
Jesuit, Edmund Campion, and his son came to England as priest from
the College at Douai and was almost immediately arrested at Manchester, where he died in gaol.

When later de Hoghtons accepted the Anglican beliefs, their affairs prospered, sustained by growing favour at Court, first with James I and later with King Charles. This eventually cost them the Tower, surrendered to Roundhead troops who promptly blew it up either by design or through drunken handling of explosives. By the early nineteenth century, Hoghton Tower was a ruin, poor families living in one wing and decaying furniture and peeling pictures abandoned in the magnificent rooms once occupied by the King and his suite. Charles Dickens visited the place and wandered around: "I got in among the ancient rooms, many of them with their floors and ceilings down, the beams and rafters hanging dangerously down, the plaster dropping as I trod, the oaken panels stripped away, the windows half walled up, half broken. I looked down between balustrades upon a massive old table and benches, fearing to see I know not what dead-alive creatures come in and seat themselves . . . all over the house I was awed by gaps and chinks where the sky stared sorrowfully at me."

By the end of the same century the de Hoghtons were back at the Tower, the place restored and hardly a trace remaining of its previous neglect. The gardens, too, were rescued from their wilderness and all seemed set for a fair future. In the postwar years the high cost of upkeep persuaded Sir Cuthbert de Hoghton to open the house to the public, but after his death and a confused period of the family history, it was closed and its future seems uncertain.

Running northwards to cross the Darwen at Samlesbury Bottoms, a lane leads to the newer Blackburn road and to Samlesbury Hall. This fourteenth-century building replaced a hall built two hundred years earlier some two miles away by the ford across the Ribble. Scots invaders burned this timber lower hall, while the Gospatrick family sheltered fearfully in its stone tower. Then the Scots ran along Potters Lane to the church, pillaging the sacred vessels and vestments and gathering them into a cart for transport north. Today a witch lies buried under a spiked gravestone in the churchyard. Inside, Jacobean box pews tilt and totter on an uneven floor, some intricately carved with the initials and dates of long-dead Samlesbury families; in Stuart times they were allowed to enclose part of the floor with a pew whose size and ornamentation reflected their rank and wealth.

The Gospatrick family built their second hall well away from the river and its ford. The family inheritance passed through the female line to Gilbert Southworth, who built Samlesbury Hall deep in thick woodland. Work started in 1340, and as the Southworth family grew in wealth and power the hall was regularly improved and extended. Although the moat has gone and the Great Hall has been altered, Sam-

Samlesbury Hall, home of the Southworth family

lesbury Hall remains one of the finest black and white medieval halls in the country.

A fighting family strong in their convictions, Southworths were to be found wherever a battle was being fought, the old confirming their bravery and the young earning their spurs. In his teens, Thomas Southworth fought at Flodden Field before inheriting Samlesbury. His son, John, was knighted for fighting in the Scottish wars and Elizabeth I made him a Sheriff of Lancashire. Loyal both to his Queen and his childhood religion, the post-Reformation laws were a dilemma for John. Nothing could persuade him to conform to the newly-established English Church and his only building work at Samlesbury was the construction of priests' hiding holes, one of which sheltered Campion in 1581. Sir John spent much of his time in a London prison or under house-arrest in Manchester.

His son, another John, became a priest and worked in England for thirty-five years, apart from a brief period of exile in France. Catching priests was a profitable business and John Southworth was regularly in and out of prison up to the time of the Civil War. His last arrest came in 1654 and at the age of seventy-two he became the last Catholic priest to be arrested for his beliefs in England. He was hanged, drawn and quartered and his executioner accepted forty shillings for the remains. These were roughly put together and shipped to Douai, eventually being returned to England about fifty years ago to rest in a glass coffin at Westminster Cathedral.

A mile beyond Samlesbury the Ribble winds westwards, past Balderstone village and on to Ribchester. The motor road to the old Roman fort runs downhill from Samlesbury, flattening out by the south bank of the river at New Hall, built by George Talbot in 1665. Until the 1950s this old house was well cared for, but since then it has been used for farm storage. The roof, or what is left of it, now sags alarmingly and the crumbling walls and chimneys are ready to fall. Indifference and neglect have achieved what centuries of Lancashire weather failed to do.

When the Talbot estates passed to the de Tabley family, the old Bridge Inn where the road crosses the river became the de Tabley Arms, a favourite spot for visitors. Ribchester lies a mile or so away, past the mouth of Gallows Lane. Almost every street in the village betrays evidence of the past, when as Bremetennacum it was an important staging post in Roman Britain. The White Bull inn porch is supported by columns from Minerva's temple; stones used to build the parish church were undoubtedly scavenged from the Roman ruins.

About AD 80, Julius Agricola paused here on the Ribble bank. Liking what he saw and recognising the strategic advantages of this stretch of river, he built a fort to guard a vital junction of Roman roads running the length and breadth of Britain. For three hundred years Rib-

The White Bull, Ribchester, (1707)

chester was Lancashire's biggest Roman fortress, housing a thousand men, and one of the most important in Rome's farthermost reach of Empire.

Belief that Rome's rule would run for ever led the army to replace the earlier timber fort with a more substantial stone stronghold. Safe within its protective walls were the Praetorium, or army headquarters, the governor's house, barracks and armouries. Because of the risk of fire, the heated bath house was built outside the perimeter wall and, as Ribchester settled down to a comfortable, safe existence, a civil village grew up alongside. Families of serving soldiers lived here, together with retired troops who preferred Lancashire to Rome and farmed the fertile Ribble land or bred horses for the army.

When the Roman legions were recalled to Rome, they confidently expected to return to Ribchester. Instead their empty stronghold decayed, and its stone walls tumbled. Although the Normans made a half-hearted attempt at restoration, it was left to the invading Scots to complete the work of nature and completely destroy what Rome had so carefully constructed. In the eighteenth century the process was reversed, the start of a mad rush to rediscover the Roman town. Since then, antiquarians, both professional and amateur, have been digging furiously all over the village for evidence of the buried past.

Much of what they found is in the village museum, although it was only allowed to keep a copy of the famous Ribchester Helmet, as the original was quickly whisked off to the British Museum. Hearts beat faster when a Ribchester field is put up for sale. Nobody knows what treasures it may hide and historians feel a twinge of anxiety that haphazard building operations or careless excavation may rob the world of valuable treasures.

Although it is owned by the National Trust, Ribchester Museum had to stand by and watch as half an acre between the bath house and the Roman road from Manchester was publicly auctioned. Lack of funds prevented them from making a bid, although the site had historic interest and was also suitable for a badly needed new and larger museum. Hemmed in by church buildings, the present museum is pitifully small, little more than a church hall. Since 1965 the annual number of visitors has risen from 11,000 to 28,000, but the curator still has to wash newly-found Roman pottery at the kitchen sink and many finds are sent to Liverpool for safe keeping because of lack of space.

8 · PENDLE TO CLITHEROE

Rising 1,831 feet above sea level, Pendle misses being a mountain by less than 200 feet. But though it remains a simple hill, its base covers 25 square miles between the Ribble and the Calder, and its massive, smooth-edged bulk dominates the landscape. Those who live in its majestic shadow regard the hill with affection tinged with awe and, according to Harrison Ainsworth, "its broad, round, smooth mass is better then the roughest, craggiest, shaggiest, most sharply splintered mountain of them all".

In myth and legend, witchcraft and Pendle are inseparable. It will always be the hill of the witches, although few of them lived on its slope. Most had their homes to the south, in the forest and nearby villages. All the same, watch the giant, brown mass on a wild winter day, sharply silhouetted against a sky of racing black clouds, and it is easy to understand why mystery and menace surround this Lancashire fell.

Under the open skies of high summer it is a different matter. Then Pendle's sunlit slopes are thronged with folk from Colne, Nelson and Burnley, an industrial conglomeration that can be seen distantly, hazy and insubstantial, from the hill's eastern flank. Climbing to the summit is a local pastime, the view from the flat top being well worth the sweat and labour of the steep ascent. Fortunately, the Industrial Revolution halted before the Pennines, and Pendle's countryside is among Lancashire's best.

Although bare and severe in outline today, the Gibraltar-like hill was once part of an immense forest, a spread of low woodland packed with wild animals and a favourite Norman hunting ground. Earlier, it saw the Normans, who built a major military centre only a few miles away at Ribchester, and before them the Saxons, and the Iron Age Brigantes. Locals use the hill as a private weather gauge, insisting that it's more reliable than the forecasts on radio or television. They can tell you how the day will turn out by looking at Pendle through their cottage window. If

106

you can see the hill clearly, it's going to rain; if you can't see it, it is rain-
ing; and if the top is hidden by cloud or mist, chances are the day will be
fine. "When Pendle wears a woollen cap, farmers all may take a nap;
when Pendle wears a hood, be certain the day will not be good".

Belief in witches and witchcraft was widespread in the early seventeenth century. In 1606 Shakespeare introduced his trio of witches in
Macbeth, and only a few years earlier King James himself had written a
learned treatise on witchcraft and demonology. By today's standards
the old evidence of witchcraft is ludicrous. What passed for convincing
proof three centuries ago would today be attributed to physical infirm-
ity, mental disorder or even the innocent, though disconcerting, eccen-
tricities of old age. But the seventeenth century was a much simpler age,
especially around Pendle, a remote part of Lancashire with a small population and very limited communication with the outside world.

This part of the country was a refuge for rogues and thieves bent on
escaping the law, and for vagabonds and beggars who had their own rea-
sons for avoiding large centres of population. Pendle people were used
to meeting up with villains and oddities, and a casual story of a chance
meeting with an unusual and perhaps deformed stranger on a lonely
road was quickly invested with a more sinister meaning, particularly if
some natural calamity befell the story-teller shortly after the encounter.

The story of the Lancashire witches rests firmly on superstitious
imaginings, malicious gossip and dubious evidence. In March 1612,
Bessie Whittle robbed the house of Mother Demdike, near Newchurch.
She stole "most of their linen clothes, half a peck of cut oatmeal and a
quantity of meal, all worth twenty shillings or more". Stupidly, she
wore some of the stolen clothes at church the following Sunday and the
local magistrate was informed.

Bessie was the daughter of Anne Whittle, better known as Chattox
after her maiden name of Chadwick. In 1612 Chattox was in her eigh-
ties, unpleasant to behold, a "withered, spent and decrepit creature, her
sight almost gone". As old people sometimes do, she was forever chatter-
ing and chunnering to herself. Mother Demdike was equally ancient
and repulsive, more feared and avoided than Chattox. This inglorious
pair were reputed to have borne most of the witches in the Pendle area.
Together with their grandchildren, Alizon, James and Jennet, the last
aged nine in 1612 - they wandered the lanes about Pendle and frightened the lives out of God-fearing passers by.

The magistrate informed of the theft of Demdike's goods was Roger
Nowell, a wealthy man who lived at Read Hall and who had his own
splendid pew, called the Cage, in Whalley church. Nowell questioned
Bessie Whittle about the theft, and on the strength of her answers sent

her to the castle gaol at Lancaster. Realising that she had little defence against the charge, Bessie put up a smokescreen, accusing her mother and her own children of being witches. For good measure she included Demdike in the accusation.

Under interrogation her daughter Alizon admitted that grandmother Chattox had tried to persuade her to become a witch, mentioning specific occasions when Chattox had practised witchcraft against local farmers. A few days later, Alizon met a pedlar, who refused to sell her pins because he was afraid she would steal his pack. Nettled, Alizon roundly cursed the pedlar, who walked on a few yards and collapsed with a seizure that left him partially paralysed. Assisted to a nearby inn, he complained he was being pricked all over with "knives, elsons and sickles". The pedlar's son, muttering darkly of witchcraft, quizzed Alizon, who agreed she had laid a curse on his father.

Not surprisingly, Alizon soon found herself back at Read Hall being questioned once more by Roger Nowell. We can only guess at the way the interrogation was conducted and remember that an educated, rich and self-important man was dealing with totally unlettered peasants brought to unfamiliar surroundings. By the end of the day Nowell had secured the confessions he sought. Alizon admitted that the devil had bought her soul and that her familiar was a large black dog, the one walking with her when she met the pedlar. Her brother James agreed that his sister had boasted of bewitching a neighbour's child. Jointly they accused Chattox of murdering four men, killing cattle and spoiling milk and ale.

The following month Nowell brought both Demdike and Chattox to Read Hall. Again we can only guess the form of questioning, but it was certainly efficient. Both admitted they had been agents of the devil for many years. Nowell promptly had them committed to Lancaster Castle, together with Alizon and another daughter, Anne Redfern. For good measure he later rounded up the rest of the Chattox brood, James and Jennet, after a mysterious Good Friday meeting, and packed them off to Lancaster.

Twenty other people were named as attending that Good Friday meeting, among them Alice Nutter, a gentle, educated and wealthy lady quite unlike the Chattox or Demdike crowd. But Roger Nowell was involved in a family dispute with the Nutters, and so Dame Alice was also dispatched to Lancaster with six others at the meeting.

The trial was held in August 1612, before Judge Bromley and Judge Altham. The following year the Clerk of the Court, Thomas Potts, wrote a lengthy account of the trial based on official records. From these it is clear that the trial was a one-sided affair; convictions were a foregone conclusion. Only two of the accused escaped execution, one being Old Mother Demdike, who laughed at the law by dying peacefully in her cell before the trial began.

Apart from the almost unbelievable nature of the charges, and the macabre outcome, the most amazing feature of the affair was Alice Nutter, a totally innocent woman dragged into the proceedings late in the day and sent for trial because of the personal animosity of the local magistrate. Throughout the preliminary hearings and the trial itself, Alice Nutter remained calm, listening carefully to the grave charges against her and uttering no word of denial. She retained her quiet composure at her execution.

Accustomed to matters of law and to dealing as an equal with people like Roger Nowell, why did she act in this way? This is the central mystery of the Lancashire Witches, and we can only guess at the answer. Dame Alice was a staunch Catholic at a time when her co-religionists were being harshly persecuted. Close members of her family were priests who had been executed. Perhaps that well-attended but clandestine Good Friday meeting, the source of so many alleged witches, was in fact an illegal Catholic service. Alice Nutter's silence, even to the scaffold, may have been intended to protect others.

The savage sentences at the Lancaster Assizes in 1612 did not mark the end of Pendle witchcraft. Twenty-one years later the unsupported stories of young Edmund Robinson sent many more 'witches' along the road from Pendle to Lancaster. For a time, 11 year old Edmund was famous throughout Lancashire, travelling far and wide and using his witch-finding gift to winkle out the innocent, who were then promptly sent for trial. Guilty verdicts were easily come by, but one judge had his doubts. He referred his case to London, where King Charles instructed a bishop to make an independent investigation. Separated from his local supporters, Edmund confessed that his stories were lies, the first an attempt to divert attention when he was caught stealing plums. Even so, it took another eighty years before the last English witchcraft trial was held.

On the way to Clitheroe, tiny Worston is typical of the villages surrounding Pendle, a clutch of cottages, a pub and little else. Old Mother Demdike, probably inaccurately, is supposed to have spent much of her life in Worston and a window in the front of one old cottage is known locally as the Witches Window. When the place was being renovated, the builders found clay fingers stuck with pins tucked away behind a fireplace. As Demdike told the magistrates, witches take life by making a clay model of their victim. A pin provokes sickness in the spot pricked; death will follow burning the figure in the fire.

Still within sight of Pendle, Clitheroe stands on an ancient site in the Ribble valley. Having been granted the Blackburn Hundred by William the Conqueror, Roger de Poictou took an unfavourable look at its chief town and decided to locate his headquarters elsewhere. He chose Clitheroe, a good centre of communications overlooking the open plain and, above all, possessing a single, prominent rock outcrop on which to build a castle. But as the owner of most of the land between the Ribble and the Mersey, Roger had little time either to enjoy his new possession or to crown the rock with a fortress.

It was left to his successors, the de Lacy family, to build the smallest Norman keep in the country but still one strong enough to maintain order in the town and surrounding countryside. Its ruins still overlook Lancashire's most unusual town. Where others have changed their character completely during the centuries, somehow or other Clitheroe has contrived to hold fast to a little of everything and to combine the fragments into an attractive whole. The town has its nineteenth-century factories and mills, its lime kilns and quarries from an earlier age. But this last outpost of Lancashire, boldly facing whatever perils may appear from neighbouring Yorkshire, is still a medieval market town, compact in size and clinging tenaciously to its rural heritage.

The bridge over the River Ribble at Ribchester

Downham, one of Lancashire's prettiest Elizabethan villages

An early de Lacy gave Clitheroe its first charter of freedom, a charter later confirmed and extended in scope by kings down the centuries. With its weekly Saturday market from which the de Lacy's picked up an acceptable income in dues and tolls, and two annual three-day fairs, Clitheroe became the centre of things, thrusting nearby Blackburn into second place. Now Clitheroe goes about its sleepy way, dreaming maybe of the times when alarm beacons blazed on the summit of Pendle; of the arrival of the conquering Normans, all clashing armour and unintelligible speech, whose advent heralded a period of murderous treachery and plunder; and the long siege of its castle during the civil war, when the Royalists held firm until after Marston Moor.

Run down northwards from Pendle and you come into Downham, a snug sprinkling of Elizabethan cottages by a trickling stream. St Leonard's church looks out across the rooftops from a rise, one of a line of Downham churches that go back over eight hundred years, and all built close to an ancient highway that existed before the Roman occupation. Like the majority of churches in East Lancashire, in Tudor times Downham church was subject to the Cistercian Abbey at Whalley.

The legend that three of the bells in its fifteenth-century tower were brought here from the abbey is probably without foundation; more likely they were hung when the tower was built. When the original St Katherine bell was recast in 1881, its metal was mixed with that of Great Paul, also being recast for St Paul's Cathedral. It's a pleasant fancy that when St Paul's peal solemnly sounds across London a faint echo of a pretty Lancashire village goes with it.

In 1558, when Elizabeth I came to the throne, the Assheton family settled in Downham. The diaries of Nicholas Assheton helped Harrison Ainsworth to create an accurate picture of Pendle life for his *Lancashire Witches*. The family still keeps a watchful eye over the village, an unbroken guardianship of more than four hundred years, and in comparatively recent times were responsible for bringing electricity to Downham, not long poles and wires but underground, so that the charm of the place would not be spoilt.

Downham lives up to its reputation as Lancashire's prettiest village. It came fifth in a competition to pick Britain's most beautiful hamlet, but despite weekend crowds it is still a small, inward-looking farming community. The beauty of this working village stems essentially from nature, and owes nothing to the slick, artificial face-lifting that passes for beauty in many other places.

Downham must have been little more than a hut or two when the Romans came tramping this way along their splendid new road from Ribchester to Ilkley in Yorkshire. But they left two of their comrades in a lonely grave in the village covered by a huge boulder now built into a wall not far beyond the Hall gates.

Strung out along the county border on the way from Downham to Newchurch, Twiston holds fast to Lancashire soil but owes an uneasy allegiance to Yorkshire. Once the boundary between the Saxon-kingdom of Northumbria and Mercia, Twiston also enjoyed notoriety as the source of Pudsay shillings, illegal coins made by William Pudsay in an attempt to retrieve his failing fortunes.

As Lord of Bolton-by-Bowland, a village just across the boundary in Yorkshire, he extracted silver from lead mined on his Twiston estates. His shillings, stamped on the back with a shell, came the hard way; he salvaged only 25 lbs of silver from every ton of lead laboriously mined. For a time all went well, his illegal money being cheerfully accepted in the Pendle villages. When Authority discovered his private mint, officers were sent to arrest him. He made his escape by a spectacular jump from Ramsber Scar - still called Pudsay's Leap - and fled to London to beg a royal pardon from the Queen on her Thames barge.

The silver mine re-appears later in the Pudsay story. At the tender age of fourteen, William's Royalist grandson, Ambrose, commanded a regiment of foot during the civil war. He was duly exiled by the Roundheads and his property confiscated. With the restoration of the monarchy he sought the King's permission to reopen his silver mine as a means of restoring his family wealth. The King failed to answer his appeal and Ambrose was forced to sell the greater part of his estate to pay his debts. He died a broken man at the age of forty-six.

Where Downham shelters protectively behind Pendle, Newchurch stands boldly on its slopes, braving the bitter winds and stinging rain hurled at it from the east. The new church that gives the village its name has stood on the hillside for close on 450 years. A pale, oval stone with a black centre set on an outside wall of the tower is reputedly the all-seeing eye of God. A few yards from the porch a flat stone, raised on simple pillars, is carved with a skull and crossbones and carries the name Nutter. If you have a romantic turn of mind, like most of the people of Pendle, this is the grave of Alice Nutter, wrongly condemned at Lancaster as a witch. The idea does not hold water, and ignores the convenient fact that witches, real or alleged, were never buried in consecrated ground.

From Newchurch a lane leads along a pleasant valley to Sabden, where cotton pioneer Richard Cobden opened a mill in 1820 and provided for his workers' leisure hours by building a library which later became the Village Institute. As an example of Lancashire thrift and an easy lesson in turning disaster into profit, one of Sabden's churches was built for £800 in the 1930s using fine stones from a Rochdale mill closed and then demolished because of the depression in trade.

Along the way from Sabden to Whalley, Wiswell village remembers two very different men. One is John Paslew, the last Abbot of Whalley and born at Wiswell Old Hall. The other is Jeppe Knave, whose grave is none too precisely marked on the map on a moorland peak overlooking the village. As a local boy, John Paslew was taught his grammar by the Whalley monks and went on to the university as their scholar. He returned to Whalley and eventually became Abbot of the most powerful ecclesiastical centre in the north. His family were still living at Wiswell when he was executed for treason in Lancaster Castle. Jeppe Knave's story, or the speculation that passes for it, goes back to Norman times, when this desperate rogue and his gang plundered and robbed the length and breadth of Pendle. When he was caught the locals cut off his head and then squabbled among themselves about how to dispose of the corpse. None of the neighbouring villages wanted the villain laid to rest on their land, and eventually it was buried far away from mankind on this moorland height.

The countryside surrounding Whalley

The most precipitous way down to Whalley is along the road from the Nab, a steep descent over rough setts grooved and carved by wagon wheels of the past. Now motorists have an easier way to Whalley and the old road is deserted, but its shaded slope is the perfect introduction to this charming Lancashire town.

Whalley is a Saxon name meaning Field of Wells. Walter Greenwood described the place as a summer playground for Roman soldiers from the nearby fort at Ribchester. Today it is a playground for thousands of weekend visitors, who throng the banks of the Calder and wander the streets of the town in search of history, they don't have to look far. Saxon crosses, attributed to St Augustine, stand in the churchyard, as do stones from the Roman Empire. Christianity came to Whalley early on, certainly by the seventh century and possibly during the Roman occupation, when it survived the withdrawal of the legions and the later Saxon settlement.

In fact the history of Whalley is largely the history of the Church in Lancashire and beyond. In 1178 a Cistercian monastery was founded at Stanlaw in Cheshire, by John, Baron of Halton and Constable of Cheshire, and related through his mother to the de Lacy family of Clitheroe. Although Stanlaw prospered it was not well located, and the monks looked for a new site elsewhere. In 1283, Henry de Lacy, by now Earl of Lincoln, presented them with the Rectory of Whalley and papal permission was given for the move north.

But the monks met their match in the Rector of Whalley, who resolutely refused to yield his parish. He was a tough old churchman, probably an illegitimate son of the de Lacy family and a powerful figure in royal circles. The monks had to wait for his death, twelve years later, before preparing for the move, only to discover at the last minute that a new Pope had withdrawn his predecessor's approval. Renewed permission came from Rome in 1297, but by that time the monks were already installed at Whalley, presumably on the principle that possession is nine-tenths of the law.

The new monastery got off to a bad start. A feud arose with nearby Sawley Abbey, also Cistercian, which argued that the Whalley monks had broken the common Rule by setting up their house within seven miles of another. Then there was trouble with Whalley vicarage, occupied by the monks without permission of the temporarily imprisoned Bishop of Lichfield. He demanded, and received, a substantial cash sum in settlement. But the monks were not yet out of the wood, for a fresh dispute arose with Pontefract Priory, to whom the Rectory of Whalley had been granted at the end of the twelfth century.

Understandably, the Whalley monks decided to call it a day and move elsewhere. If they had, the town would be a far different place today. Fortunately, the Pope refused permission for a second move and the monks reluctantly set about building their new monastery.

It took 125 years to complete and by 1444 the monks were in possession of a magnificent Abbey, a splendid building that reflected its ecclesiastical importance in the North. Later a fine north east gateway was added, the only part of the monastery still standing in its entirety. About the time the gateway was built John Paslew came from Wiswell Hall as a young novice. After a spell at Oxford, where he took a divinity degree, he returned to Whalley and was elected Abbot on 7th August 1507. His skill and vigour greatly increased the Abbey's income but at the same time he entertained on a lavish scale and the place was usually packed with guests and official visitors. Records of the time show that twenty monks and a handful of novices served the abbey, but the household employed seventy servants in addition to the abbot's personal staff of twenty.

Despite the noble style of Abbot Paslew's life, the King's Commissioners found little to complain about when they made an official inspec-

Whalley Abbey, the north-east gateway

tion of the abbey and its books in 1535. Unfortunately the Abbot backed the wrong horse when he supported the Pilgrimage of Grace, which ended in failure in October 1536. His involvement in the affair appears to have been of the slightest, but Paslew refused the offer of a pardon provided he took an oath of loyalty to the King. On 9th March 1537 he was tried for treason, pleaded guilty and was executed the following day.

The effect on Whalley was disastrous. A fortnight after the execution the Earl of Sussex arrived in the town, where he remained until the King's officers took possession of the abbey, dispersed the monks and looted all valuables. Thereafter the local gentry more or less helped themselves. The Bradylls and the Asshetons clubbed together to buy the Abbey lands and buildings, together with the manor of Whalley, for a little over £2,000. The Abbey was demolished and its stones used to build the Assheton mansion, now a conference house. The property changed hands a number of times until in 1923 it was acquired by the Diocese of Manchester, except for the laybrothers' section of the monastery bought by the Catholic community some years earlier.

A classic example of the Lancashire tradition of achieving fame and fortune from obscure beginnings is found in the Brooks family of Whalley. Originally farmers from Brooks Clough on the Nab, one of their boys set up as a cotton merchant for Whalley weavers at the turn of the nineteenth century. Also acting as their money lender, he went on to become a partner in a Blackburn bank. One of his grandsons was raised to the peerage; the other stuck to banking and developed a prosperous side line as a land agent and builder. Manchester's Whalley Range is named after his home town.

9 · FOOTHILLS AND FELLS

Until the arrival of motor traffic the main road between Preston and Lancaster was a quiet highway, passing through a series of dozing villages before reaching the county capital. Cars and lorries changed all that. The A6 was widened and straightened to carry an ever-increasing flow of vehicles, both commercial and private, until it could take no more. A parallel motorway was built to ease the pressure, but by then it was too late. The damage had been done and the A6 villages had ceased to be places for a leisurely stop and a quiet stroll; they had become dust-covered settlements, their cottage foundations weakened by the constant thunder and vibration of heavy traffic.

Broughton is the first village beyond Preston on the A6, the squat tower of the old church tucked away at the end of a narrow lane off the main road. Not far away, Broughton Tower, home of the fighting Singleton family, was pulled down and its moat filled in during the last century. The village-proper is a mile away, its crossroads, a notorious bottleneck, is flanked by the Shuttleworth Arms and the Golden Ball.

Further along, where the road skips round the edge of parkland, Barton usually flashes by at speed. The Barton family was one to be reckoned with in these parts and their wooded acres were a hunter's delight. When a wild boar decided to reverse roles and become the hunter rather than the hunted, the head of the family offered his daughter's hand to the man brave enough to kill the creature. A sprightly young Shuttleworth did the deed, married the girl and eventually came to hold all the Barton lands. The Boar's Head inn at Barton recalls the story, and a Shuttleworth descendant was the equally brave man who fired Barton Hall rather than incur the expense of receiving a visit from James I.

During the Jacobite rebellions, the Preston to Lancaster road saw the rebels come and go on more than one occasion, often hotly pursued by troops rounding up Stuart supporters. One rebel officer strayed off the main road and was killed on Barton Lane by an unknown sniper.

Tudor manor (now a restaurant) near Broughton

Unknown, that is, except to one farmer's family, who disposed of the
soldier's corpse and his horse in their pond. The bones of his mount
were discovered when the pond was drained about a century ago. His
sword and saddle bags - the last lightened of their gold - were hidden in
the farmhouse thatch for safe keeping and came to light years later
when the place was re-roofed.

If the villages along the main road have suffered during the last half
century, the intricate cat's cradle of country lanes to the east is little
changed. Few people explore this fascinating countryside. Those that
do are rewarded by the slow pleasures of a gentle Lancashire landscape,
the easy-going good nature of its farming folk, and more than a glimpse
of an historic past.

Close to Goosnargh, a snug village where the traditional harmony of
church, school and inn is still evident, a narrow track leads to Chingle
Hall, a small moated manor built by the Singletons in 1260 alongside,
Roman Watling Street. It stayed in their hands for over three hundred
years, when it passed to the Wall family. The Howarths took it over at
the end of the last war, when the place was run down and almost dere-

new from Beacon Fell, Goosnargh, Near Preston

lict. For a century or more Chingle had been a farmhouse, lacking modern amenities and yet rudely 'improved' by hiding old half timbering behind plasterboard and by bricking up ancient fireplaces.

The hall has gradually been restored to its original perfection, but it remains a family home, although with a chilling difference. Soon after she moved there with her husband in 1945, Mrs Howarth met one of Chingle's ghosts, the brilliant figure of a monk who appeared in a bedroom and stayed for fifteen minutes before growing dim and slowly disappearing. Mr Howarth saw a similar figure pass by as he was putting his car away in the garage.

Fred Knowles, the hall's handyman and guide, has seen at least two ghostly monks during his work at Chingle. The first wore a brown habit and walked along the white railings at the edge of the garden, the second was in black and "brought a friendly feeling with him". Apart from ghostly figures, the house regularly echoes to phantom footsteps, the rattling of invisible chains and the sharp click of lifting door latches; these companionable sounds are accepted as a matter of course by those living at Chingle.

After sitting for a time in one of the ground floor rooms, a lady who claims psychic powers is convinced that a corpse lies buried beneath the flagged floor. She described it as the body of a priest, bent sickle-shaped into a stone coffin or compartment, his limbs chained together and one hand holding a document of some importance. So far nobody has lifted the flags to find the truth of the matter.

Like most old Lancashire houses, Chingle has strong religious connections. It was the birthplace of John Wall, who as a young man studied at Douai and Rome and returned to England as a Franciscan priest during penal times. For a time he was chaplain at Harvinton Hall, near Kidderminster, where he must have met the builder, Nicholas Owen, and persuaded him to visit Chingle and build the four priests' hides you see there today. John Wall was captured and hanged at Worcester in 1679. He was canonised in 1970 and it seems doubtful, to say the least, that Chingle's brown-robed monk is his saintly shade.

East of Goosnargh the road runs to Longridge and along the edge of the Ribble valley to Hurst Green and the Yorkshire border. This part of Lancashire is rich in legend and folklore. Away from the shifting populations of industrial towns, country folk still remember the old tales and references to them are often inbuilt in names of roads and buildings.

On the edge of Longridge, an old cottage in Halfpenny Lane has links with the story of Meg Shelton and the Longridge cow. Old Meg was a well-known Lancashire witch and although her home was a fair stride away in the Fylde, a happy reputation for being able to appear and disappear at will took her wandering a long way from home. She appeared in Longridge when the village and the neighbouring countryside were gripped by one of the most serious droughts on record. Halfstarved and threatened by famine, the local people were heartened by the sudden appearance of a dun cow in the village.

Every day the cow ambled along the winding lanes, willingly giving milk from a seemingly endless supply to all who stopped her. Meg Shelton was enjoying the suffering and misery caused to others by the drought, and she was angered by the unexpected appearance of the cow. Early one morning she waylaid the animal in a quiet byway, still called Cow Hill, and milked it dry. Totally exhausted the animal died by the roadside. Evidence, if you need it, is a bent, grey curve of bone from the legendary beast, fixed above the doorway of Owd Rib Farm in Halfpenny Lane.

At Knowle Green, between Longridge and Hurst Greer, Written

121

Stone Farm marks another local legend. The farm lies on an unmade track, an innocent-looking group of buildings in a placid landscape. The supernatural seems a long way off, but look in the high verge by the farm gate and see the curious stone that gives the place its name. This eight foot long gritstone slab, hewn from a local quarry, carries the flamboyant inscription: "Rafe Radcliffe laid this stone to lye for ever". That was in 1655, and the slab covers the final resting place of a capricious boggart who frightened the life out of travellers along the Longridge road.

On more than one occasion Rafe Radcliffe's carved stone has been dug out and moved elsewhere, but each move was followed by a series of mysterious accidents which came to an end only when the slab was replaced on its original site.

Hurst Green village has always lived in the companionable shadow of its great house, Stonyhurst, originally the home of the Sherburnes, a family whose pedigree goes back to Richard I and beyond. The family came from the Flyde, but were already well-settled in the Ribble valley by Tudor times. The eldest son was always named Richard, and by ability, shrewdness and skill at sailing with the wind, especially in religious matters, the Sherburnes grew in power and royal favour.

They looked after their tenants well, however, for when things were going badly in the valley Sir Nicholas Sherburne brought skilled spinners and weavers into his house to teach local farmers and labourers and their wives, the basics of woollen textile manufacture. Once taught, he provided them with looms and sufficient wool for each family to set themselves up in business.

But for an odd quirk of history, Stonyhurst would still be one of Britain's most treasured stately homes. In 1702 the last of the male Sherburne line, a nine-year-old child, died after eating poisonous berries. The next in line, a girl little older and considered very sickly, surprised everyone by blossoming into extreme good health and going on to become Duchess of Norfolk, the last of the Sherburnes to live at Stonyhurst. The Duchess died childless in the late eighteenth century, and the estate passed to the Welds of Lulworth Castle, who preferred Dorset's softer climate to the unpredictable weather of Stonyhurst. For almost half a century the great house was empty, uncared for and left to fall into decay.

Many of the Weld boys had been educated at the Jesuit school in St Omer. When the Jesuits were forced to flee from France, and then from the Netherlands, the family offered them Stonyhurst on lease as a short-term refuge. Masters and a handful of boys made their way across the Channel and then up north to Settle. From there they made the rest of the journey on foot, twenty-five miles. They must have arrived at Stony-hurst utterly exhausted, hoping for a welcoming light and perhaps food and a warming drink. Instead they found a ruin with broken windows and sagging roofs. They made the best of it as they had no choice, and within a few years a restored Stonyhurst sheltered two hundred and fifty students. Today, of course, it is one of the most famous public schools in Britain.

Whatever the Dorsetshire Welds might have feared, Stonyhurst is protected from the worst of the weather by the curve of Longridge Fell, a three mile long outrider for the immense Bowland moorlands a few miles northwards. Sandwiched between the two fells lies the tranquil vale of Chipping, with the charming village at its centre. Berry's Chair Works is an unlikely industry to find in the middle of Chipping's lush farming countryside, but not as unlikely as the large foundry that is its near neighbour. The chair-works is well over a century old, its crafts-men still turning out a variety of beautiful furniture.

At the centre of Chipping a flight of stone steps leads up to a lamp-lit gate and a church that goes back, at least in part, to the thirteenth cen-tury. The village has more than its fair share of intriguing old buildings, whether they be the church, rows of spruce cottages or John Brabbin's Elizabethan grammar school.

At the height of summer, crowds of visitors arrive to enjoy its old-world charm and picture-book prettiness. They make little impact on Chipping folk, who receive them with gentle courtesy and then get about their own affairs, for Chipping is very much a working village with a community life of its own.

Drive east out of the village and you will soon find yourself in foreign parts, on the wrong side of the Yorkshire border. Close to the boun-dary, at Bashall Eaves, Browsholme Hall is one of Lancashire's most secluded and peaceful stately homes. Perhaps stately is a misnomer, if it brings to mind a colonnaded mansion with marble floors, state apart-ments and the rest. Browsholme is a country house, where past and pres-ent jostle each other comfortably and where ancient treasures can be found in a well-loved and well-used home.

The present Hall was built in 1507 to replace an earlier timber and daub house. The sandstone front was added to Tudor walls by Thomas Holt, a distinguished Elizabethan architect; the nineteenth-century landscaped gardens cost over £100,000, not an insignificant sum even today and a fortune a century ago.

Browsholme must be one of the few places to be haunted by a horse. In a fit of bravado an eighteenth-century owner rode up the main stair-case, but the adventure ended in disaster and although the rider rec-

The chapel of Stonyhurst College

overed from his injuries the unfortunate horse died. Not only is the horse reputed to haunt the house, but tradition has it that if the animal's picture, hung in one of the principal rooms, falls from the wall, one of the family dies.

A cupboard in Browsholme's Tudor Hall contains a skull of great age. It was treated with respect by the household until one of the boys buried it in the garden as a practical joke. Immediately disaster struck the family. The stone façade of the house began to totter, the interior was damaged by a number of inexplicable fires and a number of deaths followed. Finally the boy confessed his escapade. With the skull dug up and restored to its proper resting place life returned to normal, but the family had to live elsewhere for a couple of years while the house was repaired.

Between Browsholme and the Lune lies the Forest of Bowland, although the endless acres of trees that once made it a royal hunting-ground vanished long ago. Bowland is now all open fell, with few inhabitants and certainly the most inaccessible and little-known landscape in Lancashire, and perhaps in Britain. The Trough road, the solitary route across Bowland, starts from the Hodder at Whitewell, passes tiny Dunsop Bridge and as an unfenced metalled strip switchbacks across the fells, sometimes as a narrow pass between steep bracken-covered slopes, at others riding the roof of Lancashire until it runs down to join the infant Wyre near Abbeystead and, still dropping gradually, on to Lancaster.

This lonely road has few equals, cutting through a vividly coloured landscape deeply shadowed by chasing clouds. It is a countryside of high drama and sweeping majesty, where it is only too easy to conjure up the thieves and cut-throats that used to hide among the rocks and bracken, ready to pounce on solitary travellers. No wonder wayfarers of old paused at Whitewell before starting their journey through this inhospitable land. They stepped into the village church to pray for a safe passage and then fortified themselves against the harsh rigours of the Bowland weather at the inn next door.

Immediately west of the Trough road stretch Hawthornthwaite, Grizedale and Bleasdale, the last fell heights before the gentle lowland swells of field and pasture that melt into the Fylde. Here are the sources of the Wyre, the Calder and the Brock, which together with the Ribble and the Lune drive deep scars across the breadth of Lancashire.

The Brock springs from Bleasdale, near a Bronze Age settlement, then down to Jack Anderton Bridge, where it follows a secret course, its flowered banks hidden beneath sheltering trees. The Brock is a peaceful, shallow river, a source of joy to countless generations of small boys

St Bartholomew's Church, Chipping, built in the thirteenth century
by local masons

Browsholme Hall, Bashall Eaves, a Tudor house
with Elizabethan sandstone front

and grown-up country lovers. That it has managed to survive
unscathed, despite repeated attempts to build rural retreats close to its
banks, must be due to the fact that much of the Brock lands are owned
by the Fitzherbert-Brockholes family, squires of nearby Claughton.

There have been Brockholes living by the river since Tudor times, but
a hundred years later there was no direct heir to the estates. They passed
to William Fitzherbert, brother-in-law to the famous Mrs Fitzherbert
who, already twice widowed, reluctantly married the Prince of Wales at
a secret ceremony. By all accounts the Prince was infatuated with his
bride, and although he publicly denied any marriage, the union was a
matter of common gossip. At the King's insistence the marriage was set
aside, and Prince George was united to Caroline of Brunswick. Even so,

The Trough of Bowland, a lonely road cutting through steep
and barren fells

he continued to live with Mrs Fitzherbert and from time to time the couple stayed at Mains Hall in the Fylde, where parish records include a Brockholes' christening witnessed by Prince George and his commoner wife.

Also from Bleasdale springs the Calder, four miles of river between Oakenclough at the foot of the fell and Sandholme Mill near its junction with the Wyre. The river and its villages are now quietly rural, but in early Victorian days they were the scene of hectic activity. The Industrial Revolution blossomed early along the Calder, the fast-flowing river providing power for small cotton mills, each with neat cottages for

Near Whitewell, a peaceful landscape leading to
the dramatic grandeur of the Trough of Bowland

their workers. All were early attempts at model working villages, often
by Quaker families who recognised the social dangers and human degra-
dation that would stem from massive, impersonal factories in towns
and cities. But their mills did not last long. Water power was soon
replaced by coal, canal and rail transport bypassed the roads, and
Calder Vale mills were badly sited to use either. Except for one or two,
the Calder mills were abandoned and their heaped stones, hidden
behind tall grasses, can still be found close to the river.

A tranquil corner hidden in the fells, Trough of Bowland

Abbeystead Bridge, by the village that grew round a Cistercian Abbey
established in the twelfth century

The Wyre's broad mouth at Fleetwood is reduced to a narrow trickle
at its source, or rather at its twin starting points on Tarnbrook Fell in
the north and Marshaw Fell three miles to the south. Both streams meet
near Abbeystead, another tranquil Lancashire village where time seems
to stand still. A short and steep descent leads to the village, little more
than a clutch of cottages and Lancashire's prettiest post office, all built
by the riverside.

The village takes its name from a Cistercian Abbey built here as an
offshoot of the great monastery at Furness, but the monks found the
place too cold and moved off to Ireland in the twelfth century. For a
long time Abbeystead was a Cawthorne village, owned by rumbustious
and eccentric characters who dominated much of Wyresdale. Abbeystead's school used to be called Cawthorne's Endowed School, and
Squire Cawthorne made the rules, at least for the schoolmaster, who
was required to be of sound religion, grave behaviour and sober and
honest conversation, no tipster or haunter of alehouses or taverns.

The post office is a Cawthorne building, bearing a 1674 date stone. The last and most eccentric member of the family bankrupted himself by building a vast stone mansion in Wyresdale in the early years of the last century. After his departure the estate ran down, its cottages becoming dilapidated through lack of maintenance. In 1885 the Earl of Sefton bought Abbeystead and 13,000 acres of the old Cawthorne lands to replace his Scottish shooting moors. The new master, descendant of the Molyneux family who fought at Hastings and later dominated the Liverpool scene, repaired the village and built himself a fine new mansion for his sporting guests.

Downstream, Dolphinholme used to be Cawthorne territory until the new master tired of it and retreated to Marshaw. The village gets its name, or so it is said, from a Norse settler with the unlikely name of Dolphin who took a fancy to the Wyre landscape. Britain's first gas street lamp is supposed to have been installed here and, until recently at least, its broken metal frame, fixed by a bracket to the wall, was pointed out to visitors.

Local people still speak of Wyresdale vaccaries, twelve fixed areas where cows were kept at pasture. These go back to the Abbeystead monks, each of whom had the care of isolated farmsteads in certain areas. When the monks left for Ireland, the Prior of Lancaster paid for a chaplain to look after the farmers' spiritual needs. Later the Duchy of Lancaster took over this responsibility, exacting a tax from the farmers for their established cattle grazing. From then on, much of Wyresdale's life was centred at the point where the road from Abbeystead and the main highway from Preston met at Lancaster, Lancashire's ancient capital.

10 · AROUND ROSSENDALE

Burnley, Nelson and Colne, a trinity of towns sandwiched in the valley between Pendle and the sombre fell slopes that take Lancashire across the Forest of Trawden and into Yorkshire. You can drive down the steep hill into Burnley and on to the far side of Colne without being aware that you have passed through three distinct townships. Together they make up a solid wedge of industrial Lancashire, gradually developed and combined as power looms forced hand-weavers from their upland cottages to the valley mills.

Nelson is the newcomer among the three, a nineteenth-century town named after the inn where a railway halt was built, the connecting link between the much older townships of Burnley and Colne. "Bonny Colne on the hill", as the locals call it, has its Roman earthworks, and Norman pillars support thirteenth-century arches in its parish church.

Two Colne men, both surnamed Hartley, made their mark beyond the town's narrow boundaries. Wallace Hartley was an obscure bank clerk who became a ship's bandmaster. When disaster struck the *Titanic* on her maiden voyage in May 1912 he summoned his bandsmen on deck. As the vessel slid slowly beneath the waves, taking 1,500 lives with her, Hartley and his men balanced precariously against the increasing tilt of the deck and played "Nearer My God to Thee".

The other Hartley was born in Colne in 1846, and christened William. An ambitious lad, he frightened his sobersides parents with his hair-raising trading gambles. Working in his mother's shop, he persuaded her, much against her will, to take larger premises and to sell homemade jams alongside general groceries. When the new shop prospered, he sold out and started a fruit-preserving business, moving to Liverpool to make the Hartley name known the world over for good jams and preserves. His wealth was showered generously on his adopted city, but little seems to have found its way back to his birthplace.

Burnley and Colne, like many other Lancashire towns, were

133

Wallace Hartley, bandmaster of the *Titanic*

transformed by the development of textile machinery and rapid changes in communications. Before the Turnpike Act of 1663, road maintenance depended on uncertain common law and a statute of 1553 which made the parish responsible for the repair of roads within its boundaries. Soft roads were considered adequate for horse traffic, although in the marshy uplands of the Pennines slabs of millstone grit were laid to give better purchase and safer passage.

Tolls levied by the Turnpike Act improved existing roads and created new highways linking east Lancashire with Manchester and other key towns. Burnley was one of these, but perversely continued to use the

Long Causeway, a lonely track through Heptonstall to Halifax across the roof of England. After opening a line from Salford to Bolton in 1838, the East Lancashire Company pushed its railway northwards into Rossendale, and within ten years to Burnley and Colne, then quickly on to Skipton and through Cliviger to Todmorden. The Long Causeway at last yielded to a new Yorkshire trade route. By this time power looms were rapidly supplanting cottage hand weaving, machines that first demanded mills sited close to water resources, and later within convenient range of a coal mine. Burnley and Colne were sitting pretty; coal, as well as water, were on their doorstep.

Between 1801 and 1821, Colne's population doubled to 7,200, and Burnley expanded at a similar rate. Both towns quickly grew rich, switching from wool to cotton in the process without losing any of their traditional independence. Specialisation in fine-woven quality cloths delayed the trade decline experienced by other Lancashire towns from 1930 onwards. Even as late as the 1950s, when their neighbours were beginning to reap the financial rewards of industrial diversification, Burnley clung stubbornly to its fine weaving. In 1952 its unemployment figures were back at the level of the depression years. Although the old economy lingers on, fresh industries are being introduced into the town, a new revolution that may produce changes as significant as its nineteenth-century predecessor.

The seemingly exclusive concern for commerce and trade on the part of Burnley people is deceptive. Time is carefully put aside for other pursuits, and it is sometimes hard to tell which is the major interest in life, their bread-and-butter job or the fascinating ventures devised for their spare time.

John Rickard, for instance, is a printer by trade, yet the walls of his terraced house not far from the town centre are hung with delicate water colours that capture the serenity of the Pendle countryside, and the melancholy nostalgia of outworn industrial Lancashire. His paintings are bought as soon as they are exhibited in Burnley, often by well-informed Continental buyers.

Apart from his water colours, John Rickard finds time to make films, acting as director, producer, cameraman, scriptwriter and commentator. His prize-winning documentary *Old Pendle*, reflecting the hill in all its contradictory moods, has been seen by over ten thousand people. Its successor, *This England*, tells how water - seas, rivers and rain - affect both the countryside and our way of life.

Ask him about priorities, and he replies that filming is a hobby. Painting he takes more seriously, and he can foresee the day when printing will be abandoned and he will become a full-time artist. With typical

Lancashire caution he is taking things slowly. "There's nothing to be gained", he says, "from pushing things along too quickly."

Towneley's sway over Burnley goes back a long time, "beyond any written memorial" says the historian Whittaker. The family hunting-lodge at Burnley "was the residence unquestionably of one of those independent lords before the Conquest (1066) who presided over every village and held immediately to the Crown".

When his daughter married the Dean of Whalley's son, Roger de Lacy granted the happy couple thirty acres of land at Towneley in Burnley. That was in the reign of King John, and by a curious combination of civil and ecclesiastical influence the Towneley family became the virtual rulers of much of east Lancashire, serving successive kings in matters public and private.

Towneley Hall, Burnley

Their allegiance may have wavered when, as Roman Catholics, they felt the harshness of the penal laws. Elizabeth imprisoned John Towneley eight times in gaols up and down the country. Released in old age, he was ordered to keep within five miles of Towneley and to pay a monthly fine of £20. In those difficult years the family motto *Tenez le Vraye* (hold fast to the truth) must have had special significance.

During the Civil War, their loyalty to the Crown was never in doubt. Charles Towneley threw in his lot with the Royalists in 1642, and two years later he was killed at Marston Moor. The following morning his wife went to the battlefield to find his body and found troops already stripping and burying the dead. Anxious to spare her the harrowing scene, a sympathetic officer instructed a trooper to take her back to Knaresborough. On the way Mrs Towneley enquired the name of the courteous officer. To her chagrin, she discovered it was Lieutenant-General Oliver Cromwell.

In 1651 the Towneley estates were forfeit and sold. For almost a century, until Sir John Towneley fought at Culloden in 1746 and witnessed the collapse of the Stuart cause, the family was constantly harassed and persecuted. Thereafter they lived quietly, for the religious laws were still in force, and tended estates that stretched beyond Burnley to unnumbered acres in Bowland Forest. The emancipation laws of 1828 allowed them to resume their long-lost place in public affairs, but the male line came to an end fifty years later. By Act of Parliament, the inheritance was fairly shared out and Towneley Hall went to the wife of Ireland's Lord Chancellor. She lived at Burnley for seventeen years, until the cost of maintaining the house became too much for her.

The old hall, successor to the small castle built by the first Towneley, together with 62 acres of land, were bought by Burnley Corporation for £17,500 in 1902 as a public amenity. The family still exists, twenty-seven generations separating Simon Towneley and his brother, Peregrine Worsthorne (the peregrine falcon is the family badge) from Geoffrey, the first Towneley.

South of Burnley, the Forest of Rossendale is a pear-shaped tract, its boundaries broadly marked by the valley roads connecting the town to Accrington and Haslingden, Haslingden to Todmorden, and Todmorden north to Burnley. Domesday classified it as *deserta*, but Roger de Lacy converted the desolate moorland hills into a hunting forest, with right of entry so jealously guarded that packhorse tracks and later roads carefully circumvented it or followed the line of the valleys.

Whalley monks later acquired pasture rights to the lower Rossendale slopes, enclosing waste land and making fine profits from pasturing cattle. The forest owners followed suit, founding cattle breeding posts;

cows were a clear sign of wealth at the time when money was a little-known means of exchange. Their herdsmen lived in booths, groups of timber huts, remembered in village names like Crawshawbooth and Goodshawbooth.

Eventually the forest gave way to a colony of farmers, the disafforestation statutes of Henry VIII encouraging a flood of outsiders to a place where land was to be had for the asking. Some of their descendants proved less skilled at raising cattle in such an unsympathetic ground. Smallholders turned to sheep-rearing, more suited to a moorland landscape and climate, at the same time supplementing a meagre income by handloom weaving in their remote cottages. Open moorland became increasingly fragmented by walled smallholdings, often subdivided into tiny plots of land incapable of supporting enough sheep to keep a man and his family. The wool industry expanded to make up the deficiency and because it was sited on the edge of Lancashire's western linen region, Rossendale also became involved in cotton, first as an admixture to other fibres, later in its own right. Almost total reliance on cotton quickly followed, although wool was never totally abandoned. Wool felt was used to make slippers, and shoe manufacture followed as a logical extension of trade.

Sustained by its weeping weather, Rossendale rode the textile boom with gusto. Almost overnight, its villages turned into busy industrial towns. Mill chimneys replaced oak and sycamore, tumbling streams

The Long Causeway and the last house in Lancashire, built in
the fifteenth century and once used as a toll house

were cut and dammed as a source of power, green hills ripped to the heart for stone and coal, and the clear flow of the Irwell transformed into a stained and poisonous waterway. All that has changed. Nowhere else in Lancashire will you find so many derelict mills and deserted shops as in the Rossendale cotton towns, echoing as emptily as the abandoned hamlets and crumbling cottages of the old upland weaver-farmers.

Once Rossendale had a keen reputation for religious observance. George Fox and his Quakers were rapturously received in the early eighteenth century, but religious fervour stopped short of foreswearing the demon drink, especially the powerful spirits produced in countless illicit stills the length and breadth of the Forest.

Potatoes, sugar, treacle and yeast, apple peel and vegetable roots, all chopped small and allowed to ferment for a few days, then heated over a fire and the steam passed through a tube to another container produces, agonisingly slowly, the sort of tipple once drunk in Rossendale. Only a century or so ago the stills were active - perhaps some still are - and so were the minds of the distillers, devising cunning hiding places for their gear and ingenious ways of delivering the spirit to customers without arousing the suspicions of either police or excise men.

The oldest Rossendale road still regularly in use is the Long Causeway between Burnley and Hebden Bridge, a Bronze-Age route in use three thousand years ago and later the packhorse track from Lancashire to Yorkshire, trodden by animals laden with textiles for the Yorkshire market.

It has been modernised and re-aligned where the way over the hills proved too steep and tortuous for modern traffic, but not a great deal passes along it. The bulk of the traffic sticks to the new lower road, and the old Causeway inns must be hard pressed for custom. Derelict cottages, with tumbling walls and gateposts drunkenly askew, are obvious signs of despair and failure along this once busy highway.

On the Lancashire side of the Causeway, a side road leads from Mere Clough to a spread of historic hamlets. Hurstwood is little more than a mile away at the end of a lane that suddenly stops dead. Until recently it led to a perfectly unspoilt Elizabethan scene. Now new bungalows sit uncomfortably close to sixteenth-century Hurstwood Hall and its neighbouring Tudor cottages. The River Brun runs through Hurstwood, cascading from the hills to where the Danes are supposed to have battled with men from Wessex and Mercia, led by King Athelstan a thousand years ago.

Spenser's cottage is almost opposite Hurstwood Hall, the family home for four centuries before Edmund Spenser's parents moved to

Spenser House, Hurstwood

London, where the poet was born. He returned to the village in later years, perhaps finding inspiration for the *Faerie Queen* in this most beautiful of Lancashire valleys.

Nearly a century later Richard Tattersall, a lad from Hurstwood farm, went to London and founded an auctioneers' ring, "Tatt's" to horse fanciers the world over. He learned about horseflesh on the hills and meadows around his native village, buying his first horse from a pedlar for a song and selling it for a small fortune.

No doubt he enjoyed other gambles as a young man at Hurstwood, for this part of Lancashire breeds sporting men. Bull-baiting continued until 1834, in a ring close to Worsthorne church, and cock-fighting, common in much of Lancashire and, whatever the law may say, still carried out in secret places on a Sunday, was the main sport of villages at the back of Burnley.

Memorable encounters are still the stuff of conversation, like the battle between Ormerod's 'Butterfly' and Towneley's 'Caesar' at the Mere Clough . The Ormerod estates, it is said, depended on the outcome and the fight went on until both cocks appeared spent. Convinced that he had lost, Ormerod left the pit, but swiftly returned in response to a surging shout from the crowd of spectators to find his 'Butterfly' had beaten his opponent's 'Caesar'. The inn was renamed the 'Fighting Cocks', and so it remains.

Where Hurstwood has largely escaped the changes of time, Worsthorne has moved with them. Cotton claimed the village, its old hall disappeared, industrial cottages and Victorian terraces ate into the hillside. Further along the lane that parallels the industrial sprawl of Burnley, Nelson and Colne, Trawden stands high on its hill, silhouetted against the sky with nothing to the east but untamed border fells. The wind whistles noisily through its streets and the place is vigorous and alive, full of the clatter of mills and brightly coloured terraces.

In contrast, neighbouring Wycoller is Lancashire's ghost village, ruined but far from deserted on a sunny weekend. When country cottages are at a premium and, it seems, everyone dreams of a rural retreat as an escape from city life, the abandonment of Wycoller is a curious ambiguity.

Power looms were the downfall of this prosperous weaving community. The mills of Burnley and Colne silenced the cheerful clack of handlooms in Wycoller's only street. A stream bisects the village, a disused medieval barn (its oldest building) and weavers cottages on one side, the ruins of Wycoller Hall buried in the wood on the other. The stream is spanned twice within a few yards by a narrow packhorse bridge, a steep cobbled approach leading across two crooked arches, and a causeway of huge, flat stones similar to the prehistoric clapper bridge at Tarr Steps in Somerset.

Little is left of Wycoller Hall, except for its magnificent fireplace. Marriage brought the sixteenth-century Hall to the Cunliffe family, who already owned substantial property at Billington and Hollins. The mortgage on the first was foreclosed in the reign of Henry VIII; the second was confiscated by Cromwell. Despairing of the way the country was going, Cunliffe retreated to Wycoller, out of sight in a secret corner of Lancashire where he was free to live life in his own fashion. He lived it boisterously, the genial, swashbuckling lord and absolute ruler of an immense estate and the people who served it. A family manuscript describes the Christmas scene round the giant Wycoller fireplace: "At Wycoller Hall, the family usually kept open house for twelve days at Christmas. Their entertainment was a large hall of curious ashlar work, a long table, plenty of fumerty like new milk in a morning made of husked wheat, boiled and roast beef, with a fat pudding and plenty of good beer for dinner. A round-about fireplace, surrounded with stone benches, where the young folks sat and cracked nuts and diverted themselves; and, in this manner, the sons and daughters got matching without going much from home".

141

If the Christmas weather was wild and stormy perhaps a sudden tremor of fear disturbed family and friends cosily settled by the fireplace, turning their thoughts to the ghostly rider that visited Wycoller once a year. Howling winds and lashing rain heralded his appearance, as he galloped down the narrow lane and through the village to dismount at the Hall. Once inside, a woman's scream pierced the night, competing with the shriek of the gale, and the horseman disappeared and rode swiftly away. This ghost of a murderer, the butchering of a Cunliffe, is forced by some supernatural agency to return annually to the scene of his crime. As a gloss to the story, the murdered lady is supposed to have foretold the extinction of the Cunliffe family. Her prediction came true as, eventually, it was bound to.

The last Cunliffe died childless and Wycoller Hall was abandoned in 1818. When Charlotte Bronte walked the few miles from her Howarth parsonage, the hall was intact though empty. Fascinated by its history and saddened by its end, Charlotte used it as the model for Ferndean Manor in *Jane Eyre*, "a building of considerable antiquity, moderate size, and no architectural pretensions, deeply buried in a wood".

Unsuccessful attempts have been made to revitalise Wycoller. Lack of water and electricity are major drawbacks; Hall, medieval barn and old cottages remain derelict, blank windows and boarded doorways giving it a discouraging and forbidding air. In the 1890s the local water board bought the village, intending to build a new reservoir, but the scheme fell through. Wycoller now belongs to the Lancashire County Council, which produced an ambitious plan for turning it into a country park and conservation area. Unhappily the economic climate changed for the worse and, apart from essential maintenance, the scheme will have to wait for better times.

11 · LANCASTER

Only a few people greeted Agricola's forces when they arrived at the banks of the Lune in A D 79, a handful of men and women who lived by the river and were descended from the pre-Christian tribes who lingered along the Lune for a time. Their hesitant welcome was briefly acknowledged. The Romans were more interested in the strategic and economic possibilities of the place than in their reception. They had discovered, perhaps by chance, more probably by good reconnaissance, a convenient crossing-point with a nearby hill as a natural defensive point. Both stood where the navigable waters of the Lune ended, far enough from the sea to discourage piratical raiders, yet near enough to bring in troops and supplies should cross-country communications be temporarily interrupted.

A new fortress was built on the river's south bank, on the site of an earlier settlement whose name was latinised by Aluna. By the addition of *castra*, or camp, it became the Lancaster of today. A broad road linked it to Walton-le-dale, near Preston, with a spur to Portus Setantiorum, where Fleetwood now stands. From Walton it ran to Wigan and joined a network of roads to Manchester, Chester and the south.

Once the Romans withdrew, Lancaster suffered at the hands of invading Danes from Northumbria, although they left little lasting evidence of their presence. The Normans found a town in decay, the Roman fortress in ruins and the later Saxon settlement deserted. William the Conqueror granted Roger de Poictou 398 manors, including the town and castle of Lancaster, on condition that he lived there.

Roger restored and enlarged the Castle as his home and as a bastion of the northern frontier, incorporating into his structure Hadrian's western tower and substantial parts of the Roman citadel constructed by Constantine the Great in 305. On its steep and lonely hill, Lancaster Castle commanded the coast, the plain, the lowest ford across the Lune and the greater part of the river valley.

Its long association with successive English kings assured Lancaster's importance and predominance for the next seven centuries. It lost its commercial and political ascendancy in comparatively recent times, but remains Lancashire's historic capital and was recognised as such by the grant of city status on King George's Coronation day in 1937. His ancestor, Henry II, made it the county town and assize town in 1176. Lancashire's only assizes were held here until 1835, when Liverpool and Manchester were allowed to share the judicial burden. More people, it is said, have been sentenced to death in Lancaster than at any other town in the kingdom, and its Castle became a place of detention for those awaiting trial or execution.

The Lancashire Witches were imprisoned in the Well Tower, chained to cell walls that constantly streamed water. Imprisonment for religious beliefs was commonplace, the prisoners often distinguished. At different times the Castle sheltered the Abbot of Whalley and some of his brethern, George Marsh, a Protestant minister gaoled by Queen Mary, Edmund Arrowsmith the Jesuit incarcerated and executed by Elizabeth, and George Fox the Quaker, whose insistance on wearing his hat throughout the trial was a source of great offence to his judges.

A prisoner sentenced to death made the journey from the Castle to the moor beyond the town, trundled there in an open cart and sitting on his own coffin. Later a more convenient gallows was erected at Hanging Corner, facing St Mary's churchyard, where hangings were carried out early on Monday mornings and attended by crowds of up to six thousand people who treated the occasion as a public holiday.

For those who made the grim passage from Castle to moorland scaffold, custom dictated a last drink at the Golden Lion on the way. One victim, a priest according to local legend, was so eager to get his execution over that he refused this final kindness. The rope had scarcely done its job before a messenger galloped up bearing a letter of pardon. That drink at the Golden Lion, if taken, would have saved his life.

Until the 1869 Bankruptcy Act, the Castle also sheltered Lancashire debtors, where for many, conditions were hardly arduous. Provided a debtor could pay a modest entrance fee for a comfortable room in the upper part of the Norman keep, the country maintained him in reasonable comfort until his debts were settled. Twenty rooms were set aside for this purpose, charges ranging between thirty shillings for the Snug to five shillings for the Constable's room. Life was convivial, even roisterous, if we may believe stories of dancing, bowling and the annual election day that ended with a lavish dinner given by candidates to their supporters.

For others life was less kind. Within the castle walls, six and nine feet thick, are relics of its forbidding past - shackles, chains, and irons that restrict free movement to a foot or two; bridles and tongue-pieces to bring a scolding woman to her senses; branding irons that scorched M for Malefactor on a man's hand, so that a judge could tell at a glance if a prisoner had been convicted before; and grotesque instruments of torture designed to extract confessions even from the innocent.

John of Gaunt, Earl of Richmond and the fourth son of Edward III, lived at Lancaster Castle. By all accounts he was a bit of a rogue. Marrying the daughter of the Duke of Lancaster, he acquired the title for himself, and his son by this marriage went on to become King Henry VI. He later married Constance, daughter of Peter the Cruel, King of Castile. Their many children needed a governess, who became his mistress and bore him four more offspring. Richard II legitimised this bastard quartet and the granddaughter of the eldest became the mother of Henry VII and the wife of the first Earl of Derby. Such is the intricate fabric of English history.

The throne of England never came John of Gaunt's way, nor that of Spain, as his second marriage might have led him to hope. But the splendour of his life at Lancaster exceeded that of a royal court and his power was almost equal to that of a king, a regal authority exercised as Earl Palatinate and High Steward of England. The royal link endures to the present day, loyal Lancastrians toasting the Queen as Duke of Lancaster.

Fourteenth-century Scots took regular vengeance on Lancaster, plundering and firing its streets in 1322 and 1389. As one expects from a town with such connexions, it played a long, anxious and honourable part in the Parliamentary wars and during the Pretender's rebellion. Peace and quiet took a long time a-coming, but by 1700 Lancaster was more engrossed by trade than in warlike causes.

By then it was a busy port, sailing-vessels crowding St George's Quay and loading butter, cheese, candles and other cargo for the voyage across the Atlantic. The return journey brought sugar, cotton, molasses and ginger from Virginia and the West Indies, and the "staid old houses fitted with old Honduras mahogany" seen by Dickens in 1857 were the outcome of this profitable passage.

The golden age of Lancaster shipping came half a century later, largely controlled by Quakers seeking more than worldly wealth. Their ships' holds were crammed with Lancashire goods for the New World, but their cabins were just as crowded with Quakers shaking off persecution and seeking religious freedom across a wide ocean.

Now the port rivalled Liverpool and Chester. The former had yet to realise its greatness, the latter was already in decline. Yet by the turn of the century Lancaster had ceased to be a port with a future. Its long rows of quays fell silent, a town accustomed to the noise and prosperity brought by its ships had to adjust to a quieter, more modest mode of life. Choking sand and silt was blocking the Lune, allowing only ships of shallow draught to pass through to the town. Unlike Preston, revitalised in the 1840s when the Ribble was dredged and confined within restraining walls, Lancaster ignored the accumulation of silt. It abandoned the Lune and pinned its hopes on a new port at Glasson, linked to the town by canal.

The hopes were never fulfilled and Lancaster changed course to become the county's largest market town. A nineteenth-century description is unkind: "Entered from the bridge of five elliptic arches, the streets, though paved, lighted, and regularly built, do not possess a cheerful aspect. The houses being built of freestone, easily susceptible of impression in a climate so humid, soon look dark and gloomy, and impart their sombre character to the streets."

Beyond the Lune at Skerton Bridge a road sweeps to the left to Morcambe Bay and to a coastline that is an odd miscellany of tourist traps, residential estates and quaint old villages. Whatever the visitor may make of this curious hotch-potch, there is no denying the natural splendour of the bay, particularly when coloured by one of its spectacular sunsets.

The tide rules this seascape, sometimes revealing a wide sandy vista across to the Lonsdale Hills, sometimes advancing or retreating with a swift, decisive measure that carries with it the threat of peril. Neither Blackpool nor Southport can match Morecambe's setting, but equally neither do their sands present such a hazard.

Before the road was built from Lancaster to Cartmel, and before the railway joined the county town to Ulverston, the every day route to Furness was across the sands of Morcambe Bay. So many lives were lost to the treacherous tides and shifting quicksands that Edward II, in response to a plea from the Abbot of Furness, established a coroner to act on deaths in the bay. "By reason of the violence of and strength of the current at the ebb and flow of the tide", reads the charter of confirmation from the next king, "and the adjacent parts had before that time been exposed to peril, upon whose bodies the office of Coroner had not been hitherto duly executed, because the Coroners dwelt in distant parts".

But the new coroners, however zealous, could not stop the loss of life. Again at the instigation of local monasteries, a system of guides, originally called carters, was instituted. After the Dissolution, responsibility for the guides passed to the Duchy of Lancaster. Shortly after the take-

146

over, Thomas Hodgson was charged with failing in his duty as a guide. "He seems to have been a drunkard and a gambler", says the official record, "and to have been indicted for allowing travellers to drown before his eyes".

The Carter family, guides across the sands from the 1550s to 1867, were made of different stuff. In 1695 John Carter lost his life trying to save his travellers from death. Twenty years later, his son was petitioning the Duchy to increase his salary, pointing out that he had to maintain two horses all the year round, attend passage across the sand twelve hours out of every twenty-four, and that he and his mounts were subject to great hardships and in regular danger of their lives. The Duchy generously increased his salary from £5 to £12 a year.

To augment their meagre pay, the guides demanded, and usually received, an extra fee from those they escorted across the bay. A few tight-fisted Lancastrians preferred to try their luck unaccompanied. Christopher Harrys made his own way from Lancaster market and across the sand to Cartmel, his horses laden with cloth and groceries. One horse faltered and shed its load halfway across the bay. As he was struggling to reload the animal, the tide swept in and the merchant was drowned.

By the late eighteenth century a regular coach service was run across the bay, and a carter's annual salary had risen to £32. Guides tested the sand by prodding it with long staves, or by 'brobbing', fixing tree branches in the sand to indicate a safe route. Even so, disasters occurred. Headstrong coachmen refused to heed a guide's advice, like Mark Leadbetter, who drove the *Whitehaven Belle* to Lancaster. On a viciously stormy night in March 1817, the wind toppled his coach into a deep channel. Although his eight passengers struggled wetly to the shore, two of his horses perished and the coach could not be salvaged. Four years later, another coach crossed the sand in a blizzard and sank to its axles in mud. The passengers tramped through the driving snow to safety; the coachman stayed behind to unhitch his horses and was not seen again.

If travellers on foot and by coach were at risk in Morecambe Bay, so were those who wrested a living from the sea and sand. Despite their knowledge of the quirky bay, based on generations of experience, men and women gathering mussels, shrimps and cockles at low water were frequently engulfed by a surprise tide. Mist and quicksands, those great uncertainties of the bay, and the sudden hollows created by the tide that suddenly upturned the shrimper's cart, have taken a regular, remorseless toll.

Out in deeper waters, coastal fishermen trawl for cod, plaice, mack-

147

erel and bass. They used to work from nobbies, craft specially designed to cope with the tides and currents of the bay, often handled by one man and able to trap spectacular catches in their bow nets. Motor vessels have taken over, although you may still be lucky and sight an occasional nobby bobbing up and down far out to sea.

Morcambe took its name from the bay, the Sinus Moricambe of Roman times, developing rapidly round the long established fishing village of Poulton-le-Sands. The new town took off in fine style about 120 years ago, when the railway company built a harbour there. Poulton, with 1,500 souls, was an ideal spot for a port to replace silted Lancaster. Other companies, with an eye on quick profit, had the same thought and a moment's pause should have been enough to convince them that all the proposed new ports could not survive on the trade enjoyed by one in the past. But plans for Morecambe went ahead. Parliamentary approval came in 1846 and four years later ships were unloading iron imported from Scotland. Steamers shuttled regularly to and from Northern Ireland, and the company's directors rubbed their hands in satisfaction when they learned in 1852 that Morecambe was handling twice the combined tonnage of Lancaster and Glasson.

Directorial glee, like their profits, was short lived. The railway company changed hands, commercial policy shifted and Glasson proved too strong a competitor. Within twenty-five years Morecambe's splended new harbour was trading at a loss and turned itself into a breaker's yard. The rising town was forced to look elsewhere for its income and turned envious eyes towards Blackpool and Southport, both making money hand-over-fist from holidaymakers.

As a holiday resort, a pale imitation of its coastal neighbours, Morcambe never really caught on, although some insist they prefer it to its rivals. All the usual holiday catchpennies are there - neon-lit amusement arcades, souvenir stalls, fairground and the rest, but the boisterous spirit and insistent drive of Blackpool eluded it, the decent dignity of Southport proved unattainable. Even its Tower, intended to outsoar that at Blackpool, never got much beyond the foundation stage.

Until it joined forces with Morecambe in 1928, Heysham was a doggedly independent town. Today you can pass from one to the other without noticing the difference, old Heysham being a handful of old buildings in a constriction of modern houses, hotels and shops. Thousands of people who would never dream of taking a holiday there visit the town to catch a boat to Ireland or the Isle of Man, for Heysham, too, was intended by an ambitious railway company to replace failing Lancaster as a port. As late as the early nineteenth century it was still a hamlet "with no market, no shop, no butcher, no attorney, no school", according to a local historian. "There was no water, no clear and tasteless spring, the wells being brackish puddles".

One wonders how the inhabitants managed to survive in the tiny whitewashed cottages along the single street that dropped steeply to a rock-strewn cove. Where, too, did they find the water to make nettle beer, a Heysham speciality known throughout Lancashire? Perhaps the beer came later, with the growth of the town, although people who brew the stuff from nettles, yeast, sugar, ginger and liquorice - not to mention other, more secret, ingredients - insist that the start of the trade is buried deep in the past.

Local legend also tells you that St Patrick was shipwrecked off Heysham, struggling ashore across the rocks at the foot of the main street. As proof, witness the ruins of a little chapel, dedicated to Patrick and built by the saint himself. The shipwreck, if it took place, occurred towards the end of the fourth century and, understandably, time has blurred the details. Before taking orders, says one version, Patrick was the son of a Roman soldier garrisoned on the Clyde. Captured and taken to Ireland as a slave, he escaped by boat and was wrecked off Heysham, whence he returned to his family in Scotland. More common is the story that Patrick, as Archbishop of Armagh, was already on his way to evangelise the north when his ship struck the rocks.

South of the port, the jutting peninsula that swells round from Morecambe Bay reaches the mouth of the Lune. Almost opposite Glasson, Sunderland died as its rival prospered. It still does a little fishing, but only a few acres of land support farming in a marshy landscape that offers little prospect of diversification.

Sunderland's waterfront is a still-recognisable legacy of the early eighteenth century, although it is a long time since it saw a sailing ship. Robert Lawson designed the front with a sharp eye for elegance, at a time when the West Indies trade was in full swing. Lawson was the first Englishman to import cotton, probably cotton wool, and made a great deal of money. It was squandered in good living and unwise land and property speculation until, in the words of a Quaker contemporary, "he overshot himself". Old links with the islands near the Gulf of Mexico are recalled by a grave, where a slave lies buried beneath a gentle hollow. Locals still call it Black Sambo's grave, and tell how he died of sorrow when his master abandoned him once his ship had docked at Lancaster.

Like many of these once-isolated coastal villages, the Georgian charm of Overton is almost lost amidst new estates. Some of its old houses owe their stone to Cockersands Abbey, a builders' free-for-all after the Dissolution, and its church goes back to before the Conquest.

When Oliver Cromwell enquired into the riches of the Church, he got a dusty answer from Overton. His Commissioners discovered that the vicar had left, unable to sustain himself on £16 a year. The eighty people of Overton petitioned to be made a self-contained parish, independent of Lancaster, and to be provided with an adequately paid minister of their own.

Lancashire has many Boltons - so, indeed, has Yorkshire - and a tacked-on description often identifies one from another. The one between Manchester and Blackburn was originally Bolton-le-Moor, to distinguish it from Bolton-le-Sands, near Morecambe. In the latter case, the description is a little exaggerated. Half a mile of land, fronted by marsh rather than sand, separates the sea from the core of the old village snugly wrapped around its church. Like Overton, the core is embedded in new housing, as retired couples and families attracted by the nearness of the motorway seek an escape from industrial conurbations.

William Stout, whose autobiography sheds so much light on the life and history of this corner of Lancashire, came from a Bolton family. They grazed their sheep on the marshes, which enjoyed the reputation of raising superb flocks, gathered mussels and cockles at low water, and after the tide had swept high over the marshes, scavenged in its receding wake for seaweed to manure their fields.

William's sister deserves a footnote in history. Her modest home life, helping with the housework and the sewing and the spinning, was broken by a brief visit to London, to be touched by the hand of Charles II in the hope that she would be cured of the King's Evil. Sadly, she "found not much benefit by it".

In Carnforth, a mile away, nothing seems to be old. It was sited by the ford across the River Keer; its name is supposedly derived from the watersplash where the cranes congregated. Invading Danes, sailing up the Keer, must have liked what they saw and settled permanently, for there are enough Norse names to justify the assertion.

It was also a port, a modest sort of place engaged in coastal trade, and a shipyard building small boats. Shifts in the salt-marsh occasionally bring half-wrought timbers and eroded tools to the surface. Carnforth was also an important staging post on the London to Glasgow haul, where famished passengers tucked into haverbread, a local oatcake, and perhaps yearned for the wheat bread that was an impossible luxury in the coastal Lancashire of that time.

The town suddenly changed its character, trades associated with the sea and the land yielding in a surprisingly short space of time to iron and steel foundries. In the nineteenth century the town was producing 4,000 tons of pig-iron and half as much steel every week.

Side roads lead to Silverdale and Warton, the first as lovely a bit of Lancashire as you may hope to find, despite its new houses and flats, and the second marked by Warton Crag, a pinnacled limestone cliff that is an inescapable landmark of Morecambe Bay. To judge by references to her in the village, Silverdale's most famous visitor was Mrs Gaskell, biographer of Charlotte Bronte and a distinguished novelist. The places she visited usually appeared thinly disguised in her later books, like Knutsford in Cheshire, the backdrop for *Cranford*. Silverdale was no exception, and after her stay at Tower House, near the headland called Gibralter, it duly appeared in her books.

The Washingtons were Warton's distinguished family, the village probably having closer connections than Sulgrave in Northamptonshire. The family originated near Durham, but by the fifteenth century Robert Washington was well established at Warton. He helped to build the parish church, and the western wall of the tower displays his bearings: "Arg. 2 bars, Gul. 3 Mullions of the 2nd, with a crescent for difference". So writes John Lucas in his *History of Warton*, describing the two stripes and three stars that are the conjectured basis of the United States flag.

Are the Yealand villages, Yealand Conyers and Yealand Redmayne, the prettiest in Lancashire, as some suggest? It depends on your taste in beauty, but even if an absolute choice goes elsewhere, none will deny the unspoilt charm of these tucked-away hamlets. Though metalled lanes and the nearness of the motorway make access to them easier than in the past, they are still tranquil backwaters. Exploring the northern shores of Morecambe Bay, an eighteenth-century traveller from Lancaster complained of "stepping over steep, stony hills" when she passed through Yealand to see Lady Middleton at Leighton Hall, and compared the countryside unfavourably with the difficult terrain of the Derbyshire Peak District.

Peaceful though modern day Yealand undoubtedly is, the villages have had their share of trouble in the past. Paradoxically, the cause of the friction may also be the reason for their present content. Quakers have been associated with Yealand for over three centuries. They were persecuted when Richard Hubberthorne, lately a captain in Cromwell's army, returned to Yealand Conyers and became an early Quaker convert. George Fox tells of a Yealand meeting in 1652, attended by Hubberthorne and interrupted by the appearance of the local vicar "with pistols in his hand, under pretence to light a pipe of tobacco". He was accompanied by a band of men armed with sticks and a musket, "but the Lord God", records Fox, "prevented their bloody design; so that seeing themselves discovered they went their way and did no harm".

Richard Hubberthorne was not always as lucky. At a Friends' meeting in Warrington he was seized, "bound hand and foot, and laid in the open fields on a cold winter night". He was imprisoned with Fox at Lancaster Castle, and 1662 found him in London's Newgate Gaol. The Yealand meeting-house was built thirty years after his death.

Leighton Hall lies between the Yealand villages and the sea, an embattled mansion approached across open parkland backed by Lakeland mountains. Its white façade is pure nineteenth century Gothic, hiding an earlier Adam style building and even older house of Tudor and Jacobean origin. In the thirteenth century, Adam d'Avranches held a fortified manor here on land granted earlier by William de Lancaster, Baron of Kendal. Twenty-four owners have held the property since, only two by purchase, and all but one have been Roman Catholics.

Most memorable are the Middletons, lords of Leighton for seven centuries. Sir George Middleton was the Anglican odd-man-out, a Cavalier colonel both knighted and baronetted at Durham on the same day in 1642. During Cromwellian times his attachment to the Crown cost him fines totalling £2,600, but the experience did not deflect the family purpose in matters of principle. Support for the Jacobites cost them further fines in 1715, when Leighton Hall was sacked and burned by Government troops. Seven years later the property was auctioned, and a considerate friend bought it back for an imprisoned and impoverished owner.

12 · NOBLE VALE

Broad mouthed at Lancaster, the Lune soon narrows and curves across the edge of Lancashire into the Craven country, through a landscape amongst the finest in the county. The natural magnificence of the Crook of Lune, a graceful twist of the river near Caton, inspired the pen of Wordsworth, and the brush of Turner, and despite its rotund Victorian prose, Wright's nineteenth-century description still rings true today.

"The noble vale is the last tract of fertile land in Lancashire, the nearest to those regions of sterility and beauty that have given to our northern counties so much attraction. Undulating in richly-cultivated slopes, the open vale expands from Lancaster eastwards, presenting a glorious panorama, the background of which is completed by the bold form of Ingleborough. To the left, a woody and finely broken country, watered by the Wenning, is adorned by the imposing appearance of Hornby Castle, beneath which sweeping valleys, meadows of the most vivid green, dark woods of densest foliage, with white cottages and villages occasionally peeping amongst them, are presented to the eye, and appear to have been only restricted in their progression by the rude hills that arise and prohibit further cultivation. For nine miles of its whole length, that is from Lancaster to Hornby, the scenery is singularly beautiful, nor is the ride to this by Lonsdale much inferior in picturesque attractions."

For all its serenity, the Lune valley has been fought over time and time again. Anglians from Northumbria settled by the river in the seventh century, quelling the local tribes in the process. They stayed secure until Norsemen sailed across from Ireland, or maybe the Isle of Man, three hundred years later. Pitched battles between the two sides gradually gave way to an uneasy truce and unwritten agreement about spheres of influence.

Norman and Plantagenet kings used the forests of the lower Lune as hunting grounds, their foresters guarding the game and exacting heavy penalties from those imprudent enough to trespass on the royal lands. As kings slowly realised the profit to be had from cattle-rearing and dairy farming, so the Lune lands were gradually converted from the chase to open fields and pasture.

Raiding Scots were later a constant menace, and stout halls and pele towers, miniature fortresses in their own right, blossomed along the length of the Lune. Weapons were stored in chests in the village church, staves and pikes hurriedly handed out to local defenders as news of a Scottish raid was received. Generations of parents used the name of Bruce and Black Douglas to frighten their naughty children. Memories were long, and patience was rewarded by revenge. The destruction of Lancaster and the despoliation of Lonsdale were finally avenged nearly two hundred years later at Flodden. Even so, the threat of attack from across the border was never extinguished until the last stragglers of a defeated Scottish force trudged miserably northwards over the Lune in December, 1745.

For over a century the Lune has been fighting a different sort of battle, the battle against depopulation. Emigration, sometimes heavy, has been continuous since census figures were officially recorded. Farm population seems likely to decline even further, but to some extent the loss, at least in numbers, has been offset by newcomers, attracted by the motorways that bring all Lancashire's commercial centres within an hour's drive of the river.

Caton is attractive enough, if only for being so close to Crook of Lune, but gives no hint of its antiquity. A Viking settlement, its name echoes through history as that of Katti, the Norse leader. Half a mile away is Brookhouse, where a lane leads to Littledale with its wayside chapel and summertime verges showered with wild flowers. Battles of the past lurk even in this idyllic corner. A Brookhouse pasture is still called Flodden Field, given by Lord Monteagle to those of his tenants who fought with him against the Scots so many miles away at the real Flodden.

Three miles or so upstream, half of Claughton Hall remains on its original site by the church. The other half has been moved laboriously uphill to make a new home with a better view. Here Hornby Castle is the major landmark, its dark walls almost lost against sombre woodlands. Once in Hornby, the church, with its striking octagonal tower, dominates the scene. With true Lancastrian understatement, the tower carries an inscription: Edward Stanley Ld. Monteagle, a soldier, caused me to be made".

As Edward Stanley, stepbrother of Henry Tudor and younger son of the first Earl of Derby, he led his Lancashire men to victory at Flodden.

King Henry ennobled him on the spot, but back in his home village of Hornby he was regarded with awe and suspicion. His undoubted military skills sat oddly with interests in astronomy and alchemy. If, whispered the locals, sorcery and black magic went on behind the walls of the castle high on the hill, was it not possible that Lord Monteagle's generous gifts to the church were an expiation of even weightier crimes?

The Hornby Stanleys were a branch of a family whose story is inextricably woven into the fabric of Lancashire history, threads that clearly mark most key events between the fourteenth century and the present day. That the family has dominated the Lancashire scene, as well as that of the nation from time to time, was due in no small way to the uncanny ability of earlier Stanleys to adapt themselves, without too much strain on conscience or loyalty, to the flow of events and the changing temper of successive monarchs.

They arrived late on the Lancashire scene, Norman ancestors giving them roots first in Staffordshire and later in Cheshire. In 1385, despite difficulties, Sir John Stanley wedded a Lathom bride and forged an indissoluble link with Lancashire. The main difficulty was Oskatel, illegitimate son of Sir Thomas Lathom, who had been brought up as a brother to the intended bride, Isabella. Sir Thomas wanted the boy to inherit Lathom and its wealth at the expense of Isabella, but the Stanleys made their position clear beyond doubt; no inheritance, no marriage, and Sir Thomas was forced to concede.

Shrewd as all Stanleys at recognising a shift in political winds, Sir John moved his loyalties from Richard II to Henry Bolingbroke, and as a reward became Lord Justice of Ireland and ruler of the Isle of Man, a connection that was to last for centuries. Before long, immense wealth and high dignities were to make the family independent of any monarch. Some Stanleys allowed themselves to be crowned King of Man, others rejected coronation as pointless pageantry of which they had no need. As explanation, one wrote to his heir, "The island was too limited to maintain itself independently of the King of England, and it was beneath the dignity of anyone who assumed the title of king to acknowledge any other master than the King of Kings".

Thomas Stanley, son of Sir John, married the daughter of Warwick the Kingmaker, but this did not prevent him from leading the king's forces in the Wars of the Roses. Nor did it stop him becoming a Yorkist when Henry was ousted by Edward IV, although he later walked in the procession that was to restore Henry to the throne, returning to give allegiance to Edward once Henry was safely imprisoned in the Tower.

Thomas also served Richard III, his immaculate sense of timing enabling him to withdraw his troops in the nick of time from being embroiled in a rising against the king and, moreover, to receive with good grace Richard's gift of Buckingham's forfeit estates for his "good and faithful" services. But Henry Tudor was waiting to take the stage, and in 1485 Sir Thomas was on hand at Bosworth, watching how the battle fared. When the victor became apparent, a Stanley was there with the crown, placing it on his stepson's head and gratefully accepting in return the new Earldom of Derby.

The First Earl lived into his seventies, not a bad age for one who lived so dangerously. Before he died, his constancy to the Crown had brought him many confiscated estates, lost by those who had not only plotted against the king but who had been discovered in their treachery and lacked the Stanley skill at changing horses at the most propitious time.

The Third Earl of Derby came into his inheritance at the age of eleven, was tutored by Cardinal Wolsey and later efficiently organised the dissolution of Lancashire monastries on behalf of his kinsman, Henry VIII. The family motto *Sans Changer* must have been mocked when he accommodated his religious beliefs in the time of Mary, serving her in Council, and then deftly reaffirmed his Protestantism in time to offer his loyal support, and that of Lancashire, to Queen Elizabeth. Lord Derby was still settled at Lathom, although he held other houses, including Knowsley, and he lived a life of royal splendour. A Comptroller, a Receiver and a Steward controlled an army of household servants, and a large retinue accompanied the Earl whenever he went beyond its gates. "When they rode abroad from their mansion", says a local chronicler, "which was large enough to 'hold two kings, their trains and all', the happy people shouted as they passed, 'God save the Earl of Derby and the king'."

The Stanleys traditional adroitness in diplomacy and living within a hairsbreadth of political disaster faltered in the days of the Fifth Earl. His death was sudden and unexplained, following alleged involvement in a plot to usurp the ageing Elizabeth and assert his own slight claims to the throne. The brother who succeeded to the title steered well clear of such matters, spending twenty years exploring the East and the mysterious shores of Greenland and the Arctic before coming home and settling down placidly as Governor of the Isle of Man.

When relations between King and Parliament became strained, Lord Derby stood fast by the monarch. The earl was old, ill and past vigorous activity, and looked to his heir, Lord Strange, to attend to the details of affairs. Despite weaknesses in the King's strategy - Manchester was lost to the royal cause when Charles diverted troops south, and the march across Yorkshire to support an east-coast landing ended abruptly in ignominious defeat at the hands of Pendle men near Sabden - Lord Derby's loyalty never wavered, but as fast as he regrouped his forces, Parliamentary troops recovered lost territory and strengthened captured strongholds against counter-attack.

Four months after Cromwell won his decisive battle on the banks of the Ribble in August 1648, King Charles was executed in Whitehall. Derby lay low in the Isle of Man, ignoring instructions to surrender himself and the island. In 1651 he returned to the Fylde to support Charles II's claim to the throne and was soundly trounced at Wigan. He fled to Worcester, was defeated a second time, captured and brought to Bolton for execution.

As he passed along the road to the market square, his two daughters bade him an emotional farewell, which he acknowledged with resignation. "His conduct on the scaffold was equally resigned; the people continuing to weep aloud, and pray that God might bless him, he turned to them and said 'Good people, I thank you for your prayers and your tears, I have heard the one and seen the other', then telling the executioner to move the block so that it might face the church, he added, 'Remember, sir, when I hold up my hands, then do your work'."

His widow took refuge in Peel Castle, on the Isle of Man, but Parliamentary troops took it and confined her to the town. She lived there with her children until her return to Knowsley at the restoration in 1660, where she died three years later. The Stanleys looked to the new King for the restoration of rank, titles and possessions confiscated ten years earlier. The first were readily reassigned, but not money or estates, a loss bitterly recorded by the Tenth Earl on the façade of a newly restored Knowsley Hall: "James Earl of Derby Lord of Man and the Isles, grandson of James Earl of Derby by Charlotte daughter of Claude Duke of Tremouille, was beheaded at Bolton on the 13th of October 1651 for strenuously adhering to King Charles II, who refused a bill unanimously passed by both houses of Parliament for restoring to the family the estates which he lost by loyalty to him."

Later Stanleys played a quieter, but no less positive, role in the history of Lancashire, as politicians or as Lords Lieutenant of the county. Two introduced wild animals into Knowsley Park, one was offered the throne of Greece and refused it, preferring, in Disraeli's words, "Knowsley to the Parthenon and Lancashire to the Attic plain".

The Stanley's castle at Hornby was destroyed by Colonel Ashton in 1643, one of the last two Royalist strongholds in Lancashire. Treachery enabled the assault to succeed, for a local man led troops along the only possible ascent of a seemingly impregnable hill.

Hornby very nearly had its own cardinal, Joseph Lingard, who shunned offers of preferment to stay parish priest of the village. In a tiny house almost opposite Monteagle's Tower, he worked on his History of England, summoning papers and documents from all parts of the country. When his history appeared it was gossiped that the Pope had offered him a cardinal's hat, such was the excellence of his work, but Lingard settled instead for a gold medal.

At a time when Roman Catholics and Protestants viewed each other with mutual suspicion, Lingard's history was a model of fair dealing. His honest scholarship attracted eminent historians to Hornby for consultation, and to his surprise he found his home had become a source of interest to passers by. When the local carrier clattered his coach down the street, with puckish humour Lingard put a smoking hat and spectacles on his dog and placed the animal in his window. "There lives the famous Doctor Lingard", said the carrier to his passengers, with a flourish of his whip, "and there he is at the window". Jospeh Lingard savoured the joke more than the feel of a cardinal's hat.

By name and by nature Wray is an out-of-the-way place, its Norse title marking a spot where the Roeburn and the Hindburn join to pour their combined flow into the Wenning river. Close to the Craven hills and swept by their invigorating winds, Wray's tiny cottages hemming a narrow street grew out of a wayside hamlet where shepherds from the fells met farmers from the dale. It used to be a village of country crafts, wheelwrights, nailmakers, silk spinners, whose raw silk, of course, was brought from China on Lancaster ships.

Now they have gone, chased away by modern production methods and up-to-date farming machinery. Their disappearance was hastened by the summer floods of 1967, when streams became swollen torrents and rivers rampaging seas that swept away bridges and tumbled cottage walls. Although rebuilt and refurbished, Wray will never be the same again.

The last Lancashire village of substance on the south bank of the Lune is Tunstall, in spirit close to the Howarth moors and the Brontes. The school for clergymen's daughters, now a cottage, was transformed by Charlotte Bronte into the Lowood of *Jane Eyre*. The chapters describing the school reflect the unhappiness of the three Bronte sisters at Tunstall, where poor food and an unhealthy building made life a misery. Every Sunday they walked two miles to church for morning service, taking cold meat and bread to eat in a room above the porch so that they could stay on for evensong.

Arkholme and Whittington are the two principal villages north of the Lune, in that sharp dagger of Lancashire that reaches out to stab Yorkshire in the back. The best of Arkholme is away from the main road, along side lanes that meander willy-nilly around the old Norse settlement and follow tracks first made by Viking cattle on their way to drink at the river.

Whittington is not as modest, and faces the road boldly. Here the invading Scots were a shade more respected than elsewhere along the Lune, for "they were civil spoken and paid for all they took". William Sturgeon was born here in 1873, the son of a shoemaker and skilled in the same trade. Enrolled in the army, he still cobbled shoes, but studied Latin and Greek, mathematics and science in his spare time. He duplicated Franklin's experiments with lightning, using kites of his own design, and left the army to live a humble life, experimenting and making scientific instruments. His list of firsts is impressive: the first electromagnet, the first electric rotary machine, the first explosives fired by electricity. He came close, breathtakingly close, to perfecting electric light.

A rector of Whittington, William Carus Wilson was revered throughout Victorian England as the editor of wholesome Sunday reading. On a Sunday his *Children's Friend* and *Friendly Visitor* were certain to be found in the hands of any child who could read, and in the hands of their parents as well. Mr Wilson also earned the gratitude of the British Army at the time of the Indian Mutiny by establishing a refuge for returning soldiers at Portsmouth. But the steady light of reality pales before the brilliant radiance of fiction. Charlotte Bronte disguised William Wilson as Mr Brocklehurst in *Jane Eyre*, and who now remembers him as he really was?

But then, all things change. The historic Lancashire has been segmented into new 'counties' or unlovely administrative areas. At least the memories remain, and some of them, from this book, you will I hope, enjoy.

INDEX

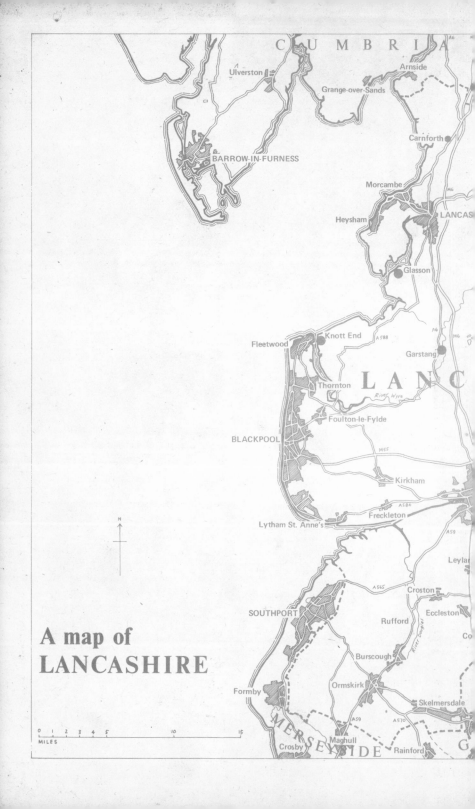

A map of
LANCASHIRE